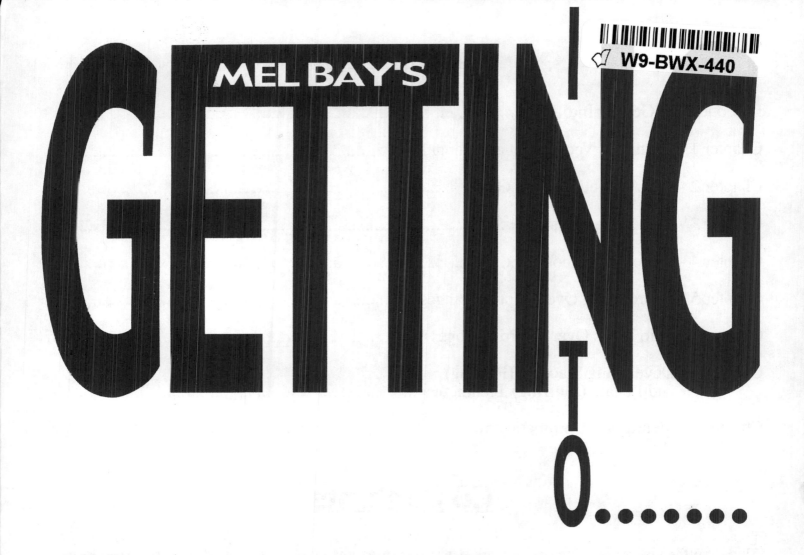

MEL BAY'S GETTING INTO.........

JAZZ GUITAR

by

JACKIE KING

Table of Contents

CD Contents

Introduction

The purpose of this book is to help the guitarist understand and perform jazz through an organized process. This process has been proven to be successful in many years of use with hundreds of students, many of whom have become accomplished jazz musicians.

Getting Into Jazz is for the guitarist who is somewhat familiar with blues, rock, or pop on any level. With this book will come a better understanding of how key center (or "Diatonic") music works. By learning and understanding the harmonic, melodic, and rhythmic sequences that are common to key center music (music in keys), the player discovers how the *approach* to jazz differs from that of blues, rock, or pop, while still containing many of those elements.

Although the majority of blues, rock, and pop music is written in keys, the basis of the styles comes from a Pentatonic approach rather than a Diatonic one. I would suggest going through the book at your own pace and also using it as a reference. Remember, practice and patience will bring the fastest results - so have fun and keep playing.

Jackie King

www.JackieKing.com

Chapter 1 – Harmonic Vocabulary and Tonal Music

The Elements of Music

There are three primary elements of music:

1. Rhythm
2. Melody
3. Harmony

When these three elements are used together systematically they create a technique of composition. The techniques of composition fall into two basic categories:

1. Tonal music
2. Atonal music

An in-depth study and subsequent understanding of these two techniques of composition give us our foundation in music theory or, as I call it, our "harmonic body."

Harmonic Vocabulary

Harmonic vocabulary creates the language we use to speak in harmonic terms. The two main symbols used to form the harmonic vocabulary are letters and numbers. The musical alphabet consists of seven letters: A, B, C, D, E, F, and G. These seven letters are the names given to the seven notes of the musical alphabet.

Tonal music is referred to as "key center music," or music in keys. A key is a set sequence of the seven notes of the musical alphabet used to create seven chords that constitute the key. Thus the key is a family of seven notes and seven chords which are used to compose tonal music.

There are a total of twelve notes in tonal music because five of the seven notes of the musical alphabet contain a note between them which is referred to as a "sharp" or a "flat."

The term "sharp" means "raised." The symbol for sharp is ♯.

The term "flat" means "lowered." The symbol for flat is ♭.

The twelve notes in tonal music are:

1. A	7. D♯ or E♭
2. A♯ or B♭	8. E or F♭
3. B or C♭	9. F or E♯
4. C or B♯	10. F♯ or G♭
5. C♯ or D♭	11. G
6. D	12. G♯ or A♭

Sharps and flats are called "accidentals." Notes that have two names; a sharp name and a flat name are known as "enharmonic equivalents."

Intervals

In music, the term "interval" means the distance between two notes. The smallest interval, or the shortest distance between two music notes, is called a "minor second." Here, it becomes important to understand several musical definitions.

"Minor" means lesser, smaller; or as a musical term, lower. "Major" means greater, larger; or in music, higher. Generally, a note being affected by an accidental will be designated by a sharp if it is raised, or with a flat if it is lowered.

Chapter 2 – The Aesthetics of the Guitar

One of the most important things that will enable a musician to reach a full potential technique on the guitar is the ability to visually understand the fingerboard. The guitar is built to accomodate both tonal and atonal music perfectly, because of the twelve-fret octave range and the tuning of the six strings. Now, let's look at the minor 2nd interval, the chromatic scale, and the fingerboard.

A minor 2nd is called a "half-step." The order of the keys on a keyboard are a minor 2nd apart. Likewise, the frets on a guitar are a minor 2nd apart. Unlike the keyboard, however, the same note in the same octave can be played in more than one place on the fingerboard. This is called a "prime interval." It is two of the same note. This is actually the smallest interval because there is no space between the notes.

Next, let's look at the universal symbols that are used as legitimate symbols for the guitar.

①a circled Arabic number indicates the string.

I a Roman numeral indicates the fret or position.

1 an uncircled Arabic number indicates the left hand finger:

        1 = first or index finger

        2 = second or middle finger

        3 = third or ring finger

        4 = fourth or little finger

All four fingers of the left hand need to be equally developed in order to execute the technique necessary to play jazz.

Positions

The word "positions" refers to the way the fingerboard is divided into sections by frets. A thorough familiarity with positions, both visually and tactually, is essential for an unlimited physical technique.

Because the guitar is played both vertically and horizontally (up and down, as well as across), both finger movement and hand movement are equally important skills to develop.

A "position" is a four-fret area on the fingerboard named by the lowest of the four frets. Thus, the 1st, 2nd, 3rd, and 4th frets of the fingerboard are called the "1st position" because the 1st fret is the lowest of the four frets. The 1st finger plays the lowest fret of the position; the 2nd finger the 2nd fret, the 3rd finger the 3rd fret, and the 4th finger the 4th fret. Therefore, the four fingers correspond to the four frets of the position.
(FIG. 2-1) Every fret represents a position.

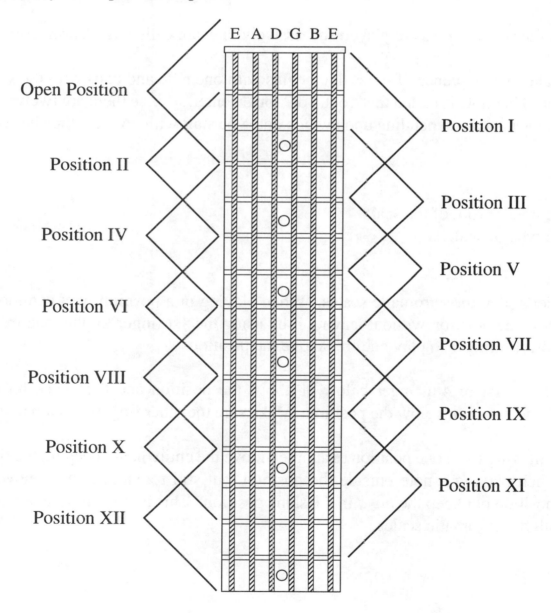

Note: Since the open string is the lowest note on the string, the lowest position is called the "open position," which is the open, 1st, 2nd, and 3rd frets played with the 1st, 2nd, and 3rd fingers.

Since any note (on any string and played with any finger) will always tell you what position you're playing in, knowing the positions is invaluable for visually mapping the fingerboard and telling you where you are on the guitar. As an exercise, play any note on any string with any finger, and then identify what position you're in.

Ex. 7th fret, 2nd finger, 3rd string = 6th position.

The Chromatic Scale

When the twelve notes are played successively they are called the "chromatic scale."

A "scale" is a sequence of notes that begins with one note and ends with the same note an octave higher. That note is called the "root," or "tonal center." Since there are twelve notes, there are twelve of every scale depending upon which note you start with. A scale then has two descriptions:

1. The note or root of the scale
2. The type of scale

Now let's play the chromatic scales. When playing in a position, you can move one fret above or below the position without leaving it by using the 1st finger to play one fret below the position, or the 4th finger to play one fret above the position.

Stretch the 1st or 4th finger below or above the position and then back into it without moving the hand above or below the position. Make sure the other fingers remain in the position.

When moving from one position to another, move the entire hand, keeping the fingers close together. When playing a note outside the position, but still remaining in it, move the finger outside the position but keep the *hand* in the same position. This is very important and should be practiced with the chromatic scales.

(FIG. 2-2) Playing above or below a position without leaving it.

(FIG. 2-3) Chromatic Scales

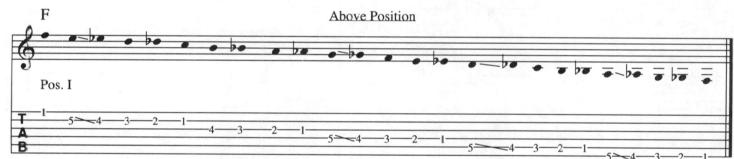

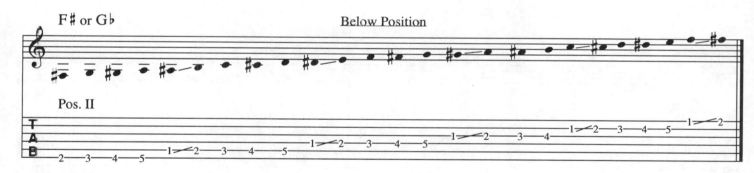

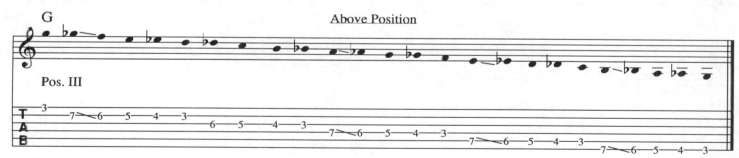

(FIG. 2-3) cont.

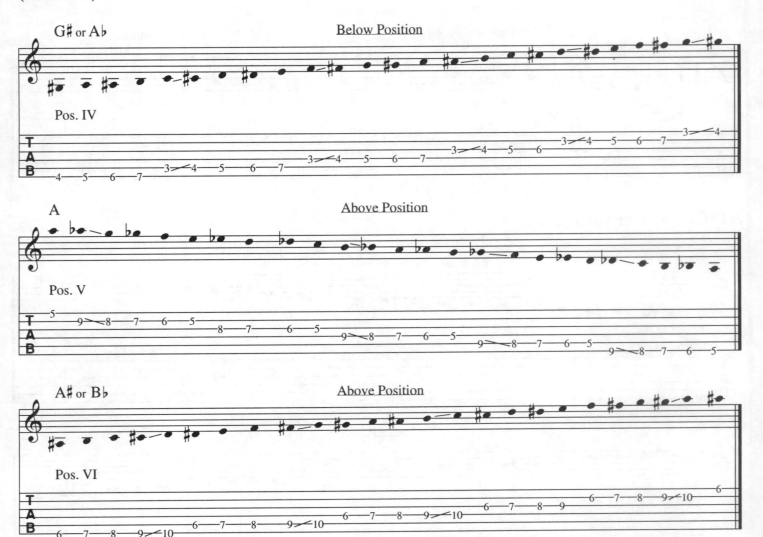

Scales B and C show another important fingering and are in the IVth and Vth positions.

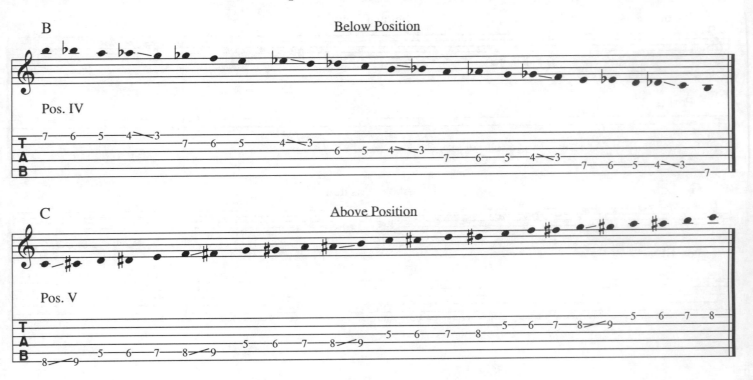

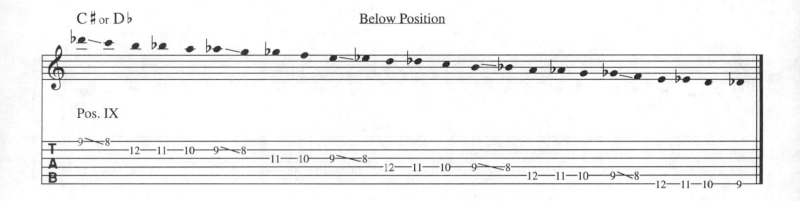

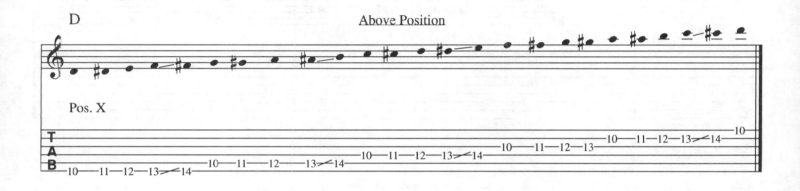

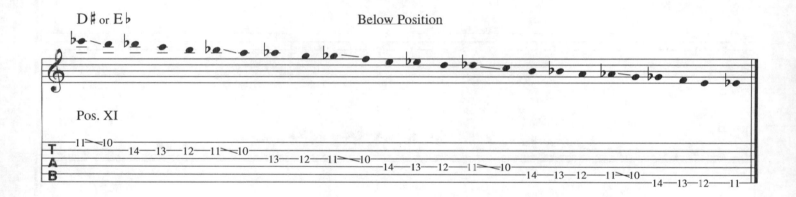

(FIG. 2-4) Use the same fingering for all of the following six chromatic scales.

(FIG. 2-4) cont.

A

D

G

B

E

Practicing and Learning

The chromatic scales are very important for fingering development and balance as well as visually understanding the fingerboard. Chromaticism plays a large part in jazz improvisation. It is also an atonal technique that has been used for hundreds of years by great composers and players as a way of stretching out and "playing outside," as will be discussed later. Be sure to use the marked fingerings and positions when practicing these scales.

Etude 1 - Chromatic

Chapter 3 – Key Center Music

The Major 2nd Interval

The major 2nd interval is the next interval after the minor 2nd and is one whole step (or two frets on the guitar). When the minor 2nd and major 2nd intervals are put together in a fixed sequence they form the "Ionian Mode," or the Major scale for the compositional technique known as "tonal music," or music in keys.

The Major Scale, Ionian Mode, Diatonic Scale

In figure (3-1) notice how the scale is put together with major and minor 2nds. Follow the positions and fingerings closely for the four primary forms of the major scale (fig. 3-2). Transpose the four forms to the other remaining keys.

When all four forms are played in all fifteen keys, each form is played in all twelve positions. Try to get to the point where you can play all four forms in every key in five or ten minutes. This is very important in acquiring a visual knowledge and understanding of the fingerboard, as well as key center music.

(FIG. 3-1) Using Minor and Major 2nds to Create the Major Scale

The Major Scale (Diatonic Scale, Ionian Mode)

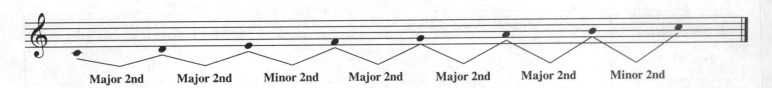

(FIG. 3-2) The Four Primary Forms of the Major Scale (C Major)

Form 1

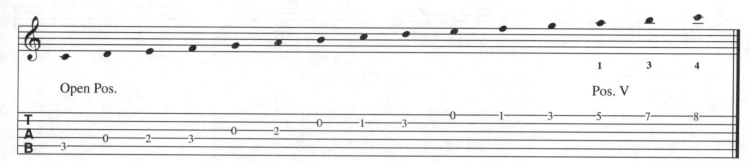

Form 2

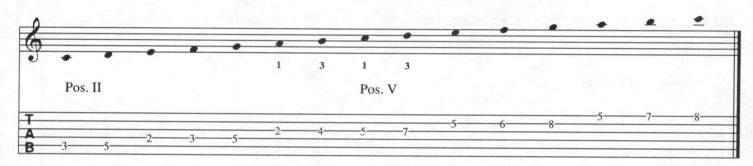

Form 3

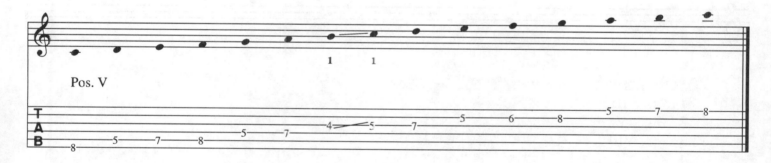

Form 4

(FIG. 3-3) The Four Major Scale Forms for the Other Fourteen Keys

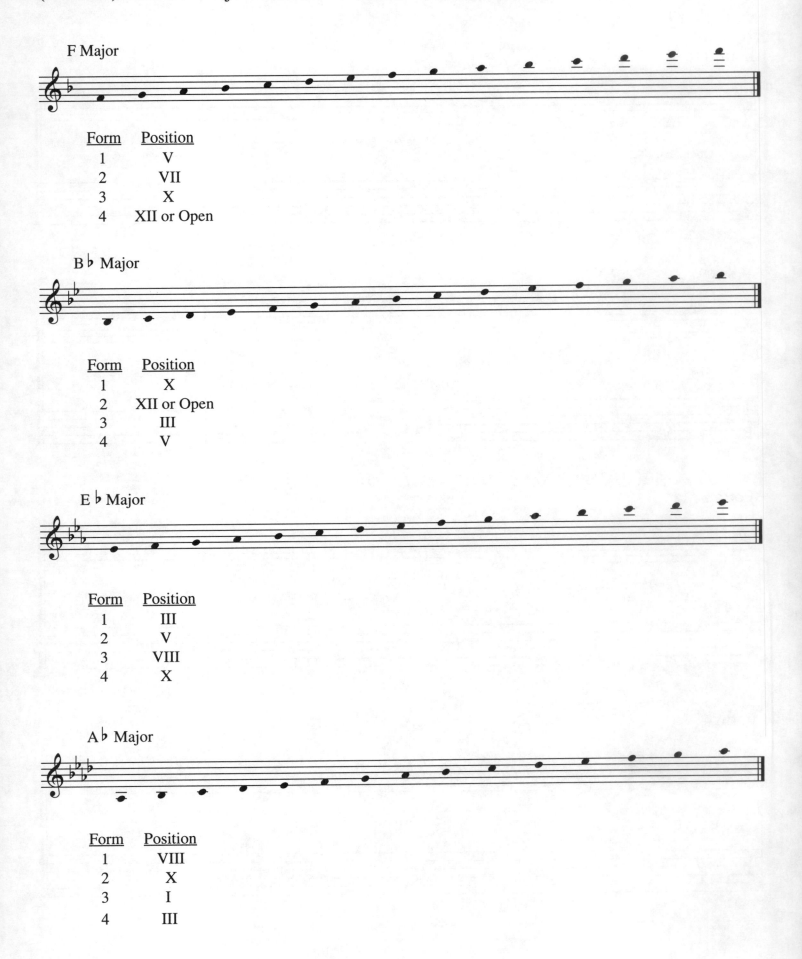

F Major

Form	Position
1	V
2	VII
3	X
4	XII or Open

B♭ Major

Form	Position
1	X
2	XII or Open
3	III
4	V

E♭ Major

Form	Position
1	III
2	V
3	VIII
4	X

A♭ Major

Form	Position
1	VIII
2	X
3	I
4	III

D♭ Major

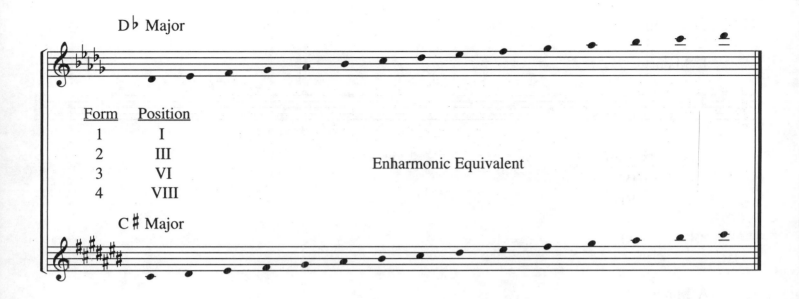

Form	Position
1	I
2	III
3	VI
4	VIII

Enharmonic Equivalent

C♯ Major

G♭ Major

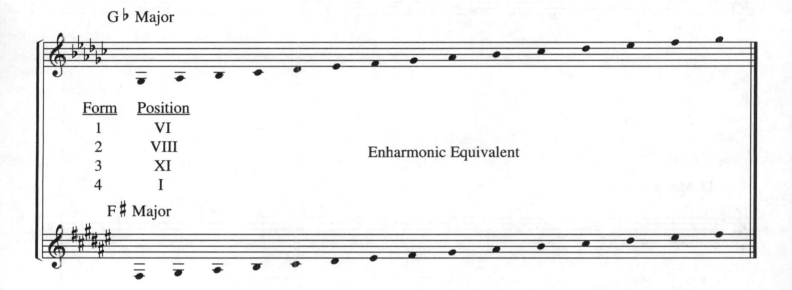

Form	Position
1	VI
2	VIII
3	XI
4	I

Enharmonic Equivalent

F♯ Major

C♭ Major

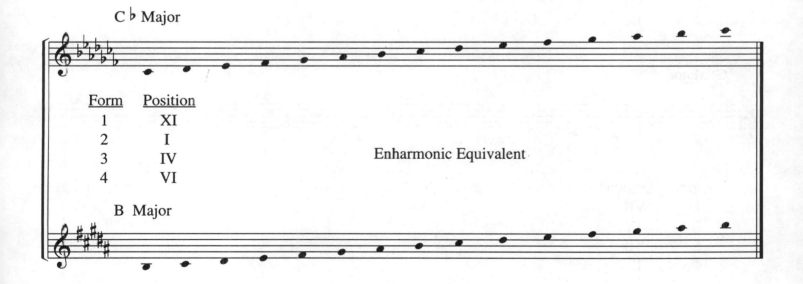

Form	Position
1	XI
2	I
3	IV
4	VI

Enharmonic Equivalent

B Major

(FIG. 3-3) cont.

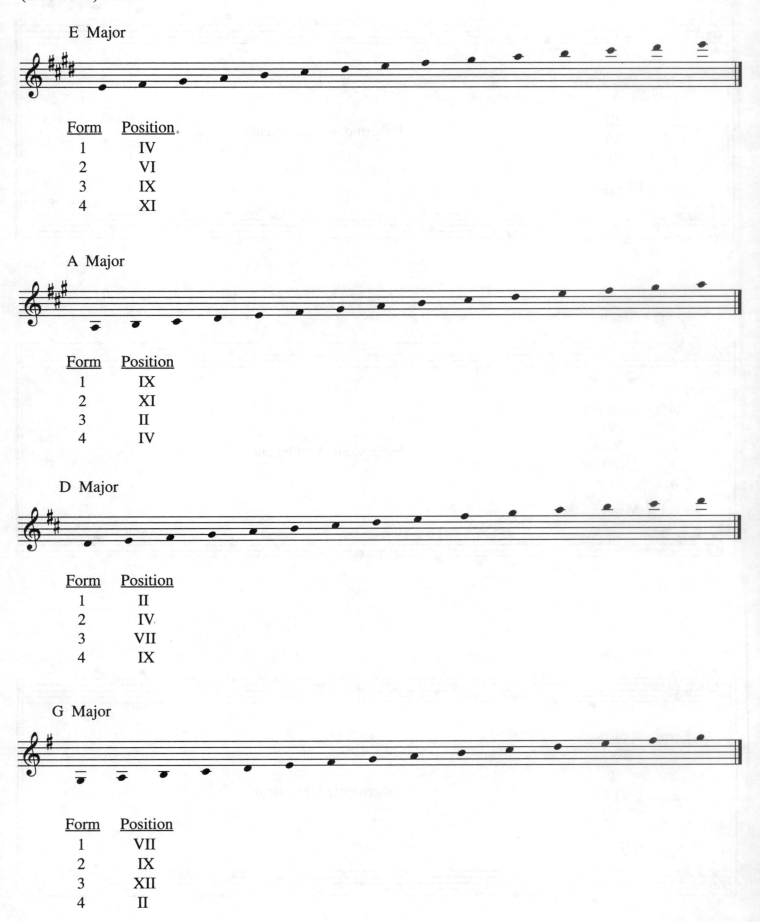

E Major

Form	Position
1	IV
2	VI
3	IX
4	XI

A Major

Form	Position
1	IX
2	XI
3	II
4	IV

D Major

Form	Position
1	II
2	IV
3	VII
4	IX

G Major

Form	Position
1	VII
2	IX
3	XII
4	II

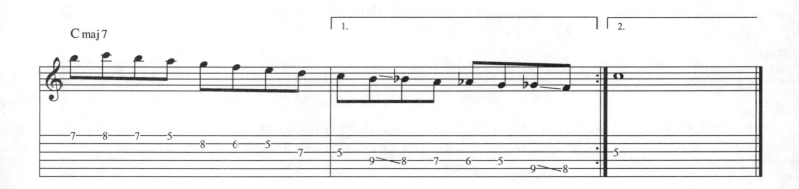

The Relative Minor Key

Each of the fifteen major keys has a "relative minor" key. The "relative minor" key has the same key signature as its relative major key, which means it is composed of the same seven notes as its relative major key. The relative minor scale starts on the sixth note of the major scale. It is also known as the "natural minor" scale, or the Aeolian mode.

Follow the same process when learning the relative minor scale forms as the major scale forms (see fig. 3-4, 3-5, 3-6 and 3-7). Memorize the key signatures for all of the major and minor keys.

(FIG. 3-4) The Relative Minor Scale (Natural Minor, Aoelian Mode)

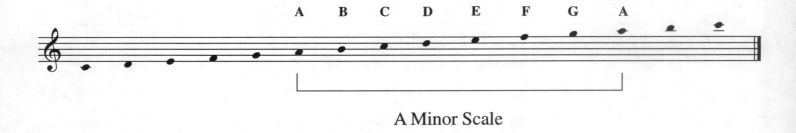

A Minor Scale

(FIG. 3-5) Using Minor and Major 2nds to Create the Minor scale

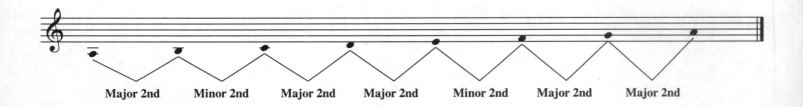

(FIG. 3-6) The Four Primary Forms of the Relative Minor Scale (A Minor)

Form 1

Form 2

Form 3

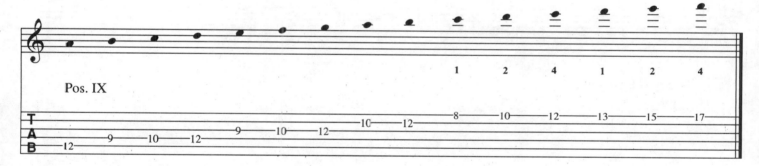

Form 4

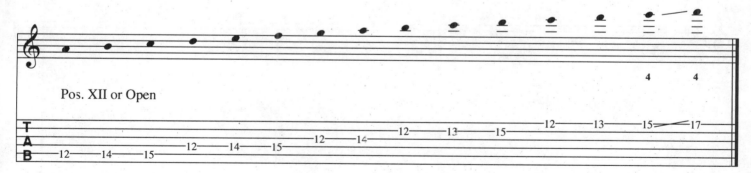

(FIG. 3-7) The Four Relative Minor Scale Forms for the Other Fourteen Keys

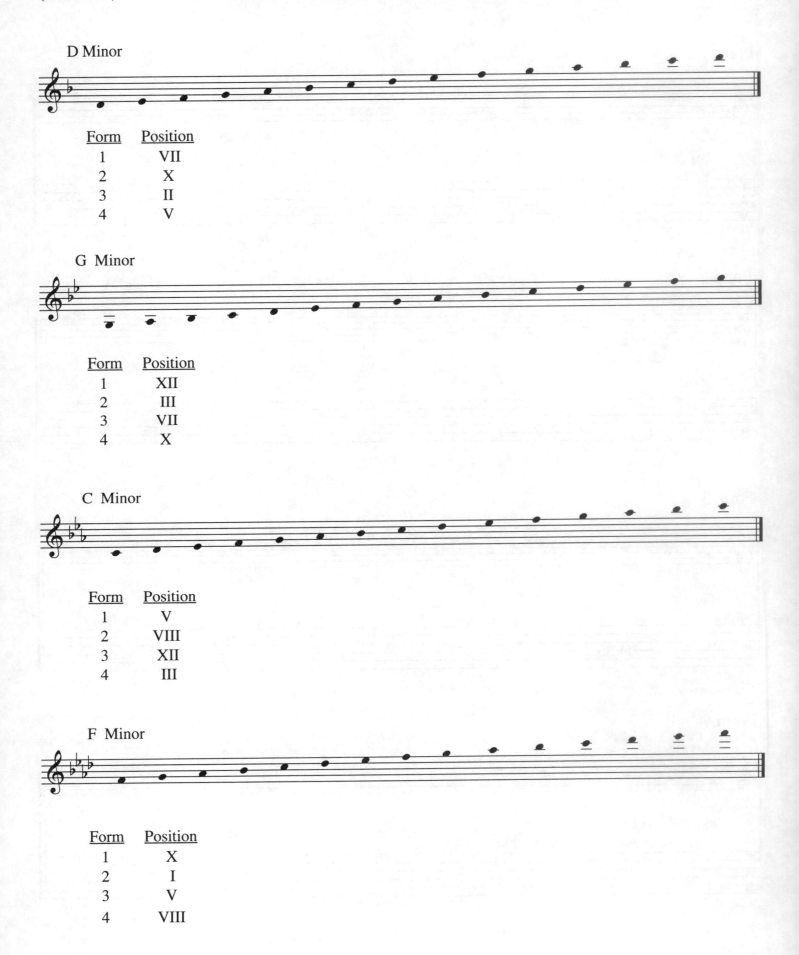

D Minor

Form	Position
1	VII
2	X
3	II
4	V

G Minor

Form	Position
1	XII
2	III
3	VII
4	X

C Minor

Form	Position
1	V
2	VIII
3	XII
4	III

F Minor

Form	Position
1	X
2	I
3	V
4	VIII

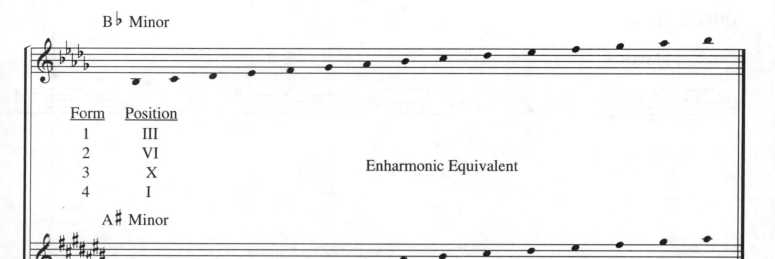

B♭ Minor

Form	Position
1	III
2	VI
3	X
4	I

Enharmonic Equivalent

A♯ Minor

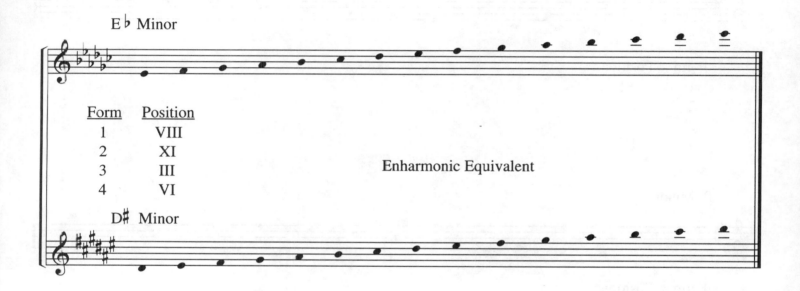

E♭ Minor

Form	Position
1	VIII
2	XI
3	III
4	VI

Enharmonic Equivalent

D♯ Minor

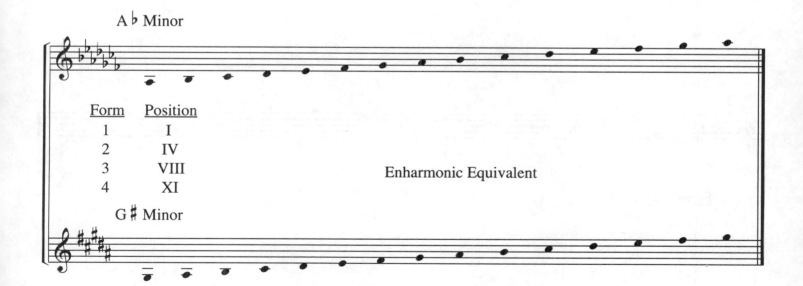

A♭ Minor

Form	Position
1	I
2	IV
3	VIII
4	XI

Enharmonic Equivalent

G♯ Minor

(FIG. 3-7) cont.

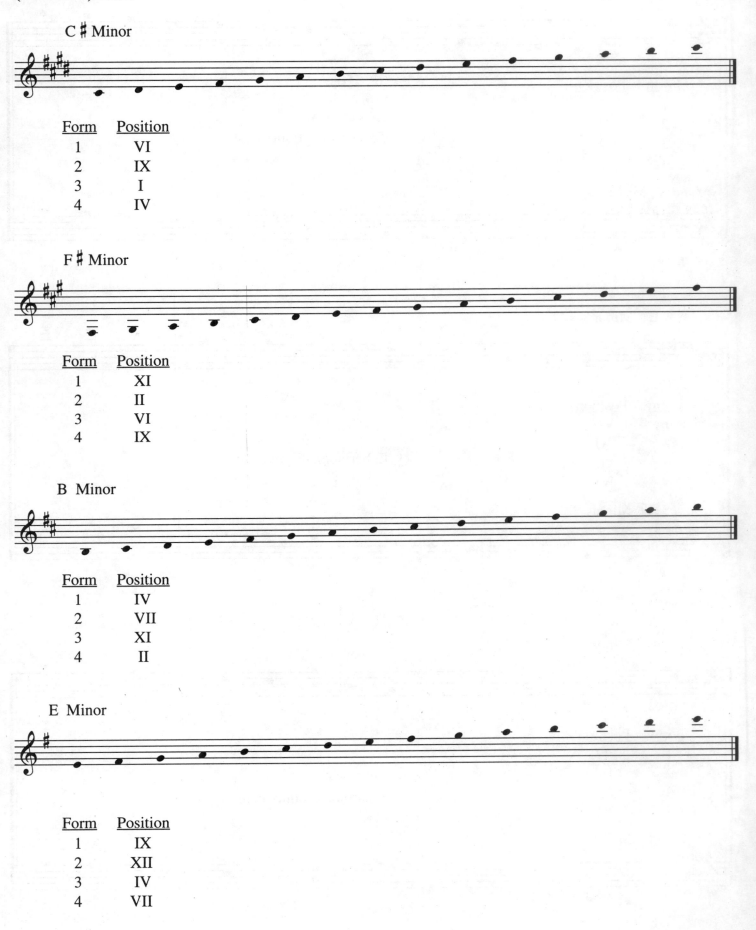

C# Minor

Form	Position
1	VI
2	IX
3	I
4	IV

F# Minor

Form	Position
1	XI
2	II
3	VI
4	IX

B Minor

Form	Position
1	IV
2	VII
3	XI
4	II

E Minor

Form	Position
1	IX
2	XII
3	IV
4	VII

Although there are more forms and positions in which the thirty major and minor scales may be played, these eight forms consolidate the essential fingerings and natural positions for the scales and keys on the fingerboard, and are most efficient in developing the technique.

Etude 3 - Minor Scale Chromatic Combination

The notes in the major scale are called the "degrees" of the scale and are numbered 1 through 7, with 8 through 15 covering a second octave. Each degree of the scale names three things that are essential to tonal music and jazz:

1. A note

2. A chord

3. A mode

Chapter 4 – Diatonic Harmony

Thirds

The next interval above the major 2nd is the "minor 3rd" (one-and-a-half steps or three frets). This interval is followed by the "major 3rd" (two steps or four frets). Together, these intervals are known as "thirds." Thirds are the most important interval used in creating harmony in tonal music. When thirds are put together, or stacked, they form the seven chords that create the key. Thirds put together form four chord types, or triads:

Major triad = major 3rd + minor 3rd

Minor triad = minor 3rd + major 3rd

Diminished triad = minor 3rd + minor 3rd

Augmented triad = major 3rd + major 3rd

The symbols used to name the seven chords of the major key are:

I = the one major or major one

ii = the two minor or minor two

iii = the three minor or minor three

IV = the four major or major four

V = the five major or major five

vi = the six minor or minor six

vii° = the seven diminished

(FIG. 4-1) Major, Minor and Diminished Triads

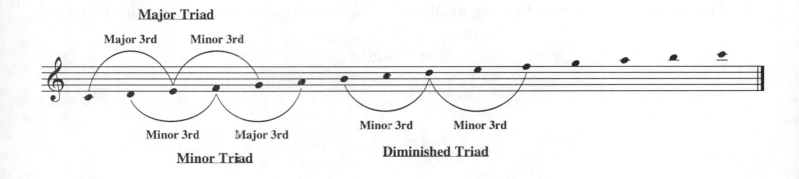

By taking each degree of the scale and adding two notes, each a third apart (every other note), we form the seven chords of the key.

(FIG. 4-2) The Seven Chords of the Major Key

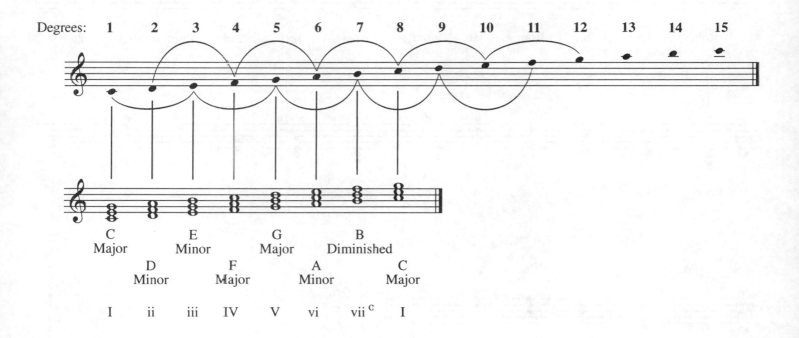

Inversions

A chord may be inverted by moving the bottom note of the chord to the top, thus inverting the chord without interrupting the numerical order of the chord tones. Inversions of the triads are:

Root Position

1st Inversion

2nd Inversion

(FIG. 4-3) Triad Inversions (C Major)

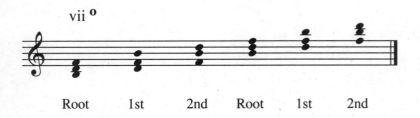

The third is the first natural harmony part to be added to a melody in diatonic music.

(FIG. 4-4)

Third Below the Melody

Third Above the Melody

Here are three things to incorporate into your practicing. Do them at your own pace; don't rush.

1. Play and practice all seven triads and their inversions for all of the major and minor keys.

2. Practice all of the major and minor scales in 3rds.

3. Harmonize a simple melody in thirds.

Etude 4 - Melody in Thirds

Four-Voice 7th Chords

The "voicing" of a chord is the arrangement of the chord tones from low to high. By adding another 3rd to the triads we create "four-voice" chords. These chords all become "7th" chords. 7th chords are the most important chords in jazz.

(FIG. 4-5)

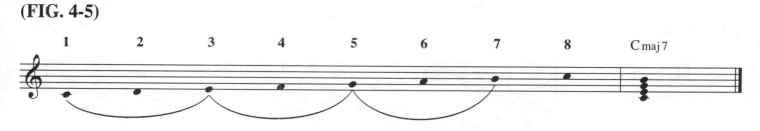

The 7th chord is created by adding another 3rd to the triad.

Chord Construction

At this point it becomes important to understand how chords are constructed. The construction of a chord is defined from the root note's major scale. (Ex. All C chords are constructed and named from the C major scale.) The scale degree numbers are used to define the chords.

(FIG. 4-6)

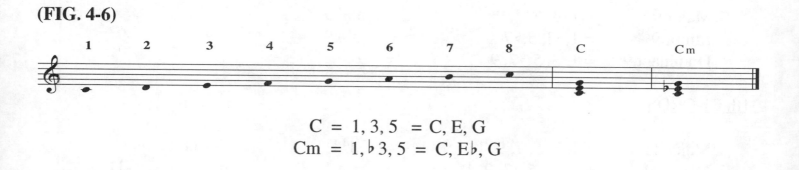

$$C = 1, 3, 5 = C, E, G$$
$$Cm = 1, \flat 3, 5 = C, E\flat, G$$

The following is a chart of how chords are constructed and named. A chord will have two descriptions:

1. The letter or root name

2. The type of chord (Ex. C maj7)

(FIG. 4-7) The Construction of Chords

TRIADS

Major	= 1, 3, 5	= M	maj	
Minor	= 1, ♭3, 5	= m	min	
Diminished	= 1, ♭3, ♭5	= o		
Augmented	= 1, 3, ♯5	= +	aug	

6th CHORDS

Major 6	= 1, 3, 5, 6	= 6		
Minor 6	= 1, ♭3, 5, 6	= min 6	m6	-6

7th CHORDS

Major 7	= 1, 3, 5, 7	= maj 7	M7	△7
Minor 7	= 1, ♭3, 5, ♭7	= min 7	m7	-7
Dominant 7	= 1, 3, 5, ♭7	= 7		
Min 7♭5 (half diminished)	= 1, ♭3, ♭5, ♭7	= -7♭5	m7♭5	ø7
Diminished 7	= 1, ♭3, ♭5, ♭♭7	= dim 7	°7	
Augmented 7	= 1, 3, ♯5, ♭7	= aug 7	+7	7♯5

9th CHORDS

Major 9	= 1, 3, 5, 7, 9	= maj 9	M9	
Minor 9	= 1, ♭3, 5, ♭7, 9	= min 9	m9	-9
Dominant 9	= 1, 3, 5, ♭7, 9	= 9		

11th CHORDS

Major 11	= 1, 3, 5, 7, 9, 11	= M11	maj11	
Minor 11	= 1, ♭3, 5, ♭7, 9, 11	= min 11	m11	-11
Dominant 11	= 1, 3, 5, ♭7, 9, 11	= 11		

13th CHORDS

Major 13	= 1, 3, 5, 7, 9, 11, 13	= M13	maj 13	
Minor 13	= 1, ♭3, 5, ♭7, 9, 11, 13	= m13	-13	min13
Dominant 13	= 1, 3, 5, ♭7, 9, 11, 13	= 13		

SUSPENDED CHORDS

Suspended 2	= 1, 2, 5	=	sus 2		
Suspended 4	= 1, 4, 5	=	sus	sus 4	
Minor Add 4	= 1, ♭3, 4, 5	=	min sus 4	-sus 4	
Add 2	= 1, 2, 3, 5	=	add 2		

When chords are composed of four or more notes, one or more of the notes may be omitted, such as in the case of 9th, 11th, or 13th chords. The omitted notes are usually the 5, 9, 11, 13, or even the root, dependng on the chord. More will be discussed on this later.

ALTERED CHORDS

Maj 7♭5	= 1, 3, ♭5, 7	=	maj7♭5	M7♭5	△♭5
Dom 7♭5	= 1, 3, ♭5, ♭7	=	7♭5		
Maj 7♯5	= 1, 3, ♯5, 7	=	maj7♯5	△♯5	M7♯5
Min 7♯5	= 1, ♭3, ♯5, ♭7	=	min 7♯5	-7♯5	
Dom 7♭9	= 1, 3, 5, ♭7, ♭9	=	7♭9		
Dom 7♯9	= 1, 3, 5, ♭7, ♯9	=	7♯9		

Other combinations of altered chords include ♯5, ♭9; ♭5, ♯9; ♯5, ♯9; ♭5, ♭9; min (△ 7), etc. These are usually dominant chords.

Let's move back now to the 7 chords in the key and look at them as four-voice chords or 7th chords.

(FIG. 4-8) Major Key 7th Chords

	I maj7	ii m7	iii m7	IVmaj7	V7	vi m7	vii m7♭5
C:	C maj7	D m7	E m7	F maj7	G7	A m7	B m7♭5
F:	F maj7	G m7	A m7	B♭maj7	C 7	D m7	E m7♭5
B♭:	B♭maj7	C m7	D m7	E♭maj7	F 7	G m7	A m7♭5
E♭:	E♭maj7	F m7	G m7	A♭maj7	B♭7	C m7	D m7♭5
A♭:	A♭maj7	B♭m7	C m7	D♭maj7	E♭7	F m7	G m7♭5
D♭:	D♭maj7	E♭m7	F m7	G♭maj7	A♭7	B♭m7	C m7♭5
C♯:	C♯maj7	D♯m7	E♯m7	F♯maj7	G♯7	A♯m7	B♯m7♭5
G♭:	G♭maj7	A♭m7	B♭m7	C♭maj7	D♭7	E♭m7	F m7♭5
F♯:	F♯maj7	G♯m7	A♯m7	B maj7	C♯7	D♯m7	E♯m7♭5
C♭:	C♭maj7	D♭m7	E♭m7	F♭maj7	G♭7	A♭m7	B♭m7♭5
B:	B maj7	C♯m7	D♯m7	E maj7	F♯7	G♯m7	A♯m7♭5
E:	E maj7	F♯m7	G♯m7	A maj7	B 7	C♯m7	D♯m7♭5
A:	Amaj7	Bm7	C♯m7	Dmaj7	E 7	F♯m7	G♯m7♭5
D:	Dmaj7	E m7	F♯m7	G maj7	A7	B m7	C♯m7♭5
G:	Gmaj7	Am7	B m7	Cmaj7	D7	E m7	F♯m7♭5

Here are three harmonized scales. All the chords are the same voicing (1,5,7,3). The chord scales are using all four-voice 7th chords.

(FIG. 4-9)

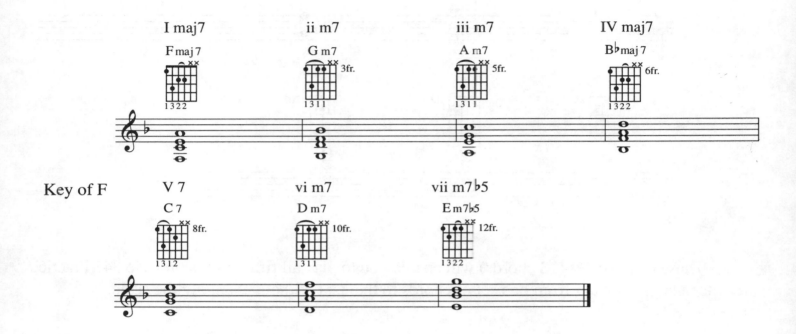

Key of F

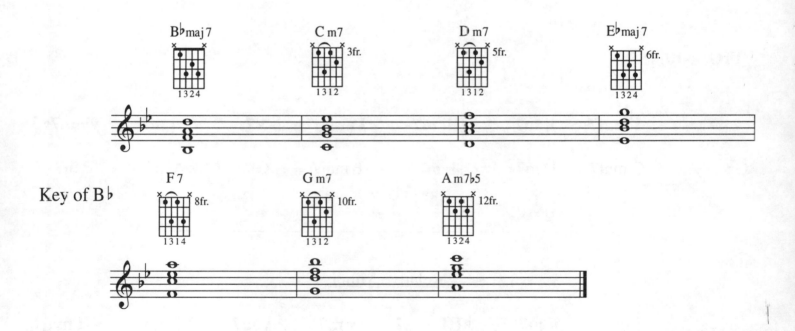

Key of B♭

35

(FIG. 4-9) cont.

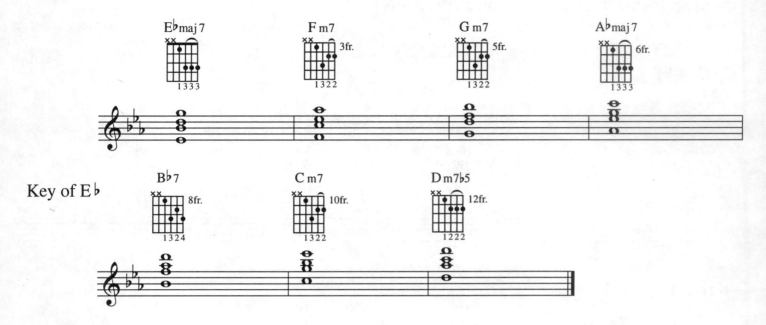

Key of E♭

These three scales (12 chords) will enable you to play all fifteen keys on page 34. Practice all fifteen keys, moving from one set of chords to the next without changing the scale.

Practice the relative minor keys as well. Remember that the relative minor key starts on the vi m7 chord and follows the chords back to the vi m7 chord.

(FIG. 4-10)

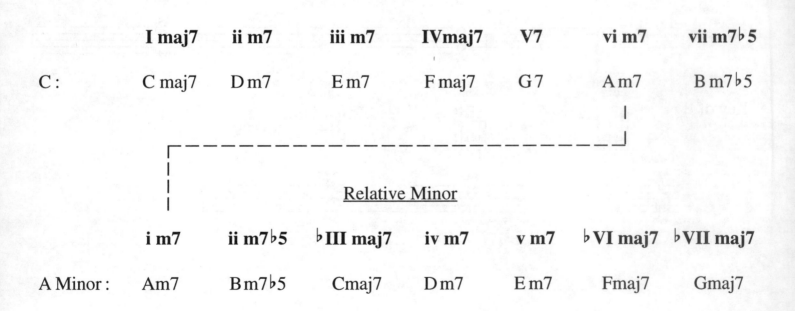

The guitar is second only to the piano in its range. Because of the six strings tuned primarily in intervals of fourths, some chord voicings that are close together on the piano are farther apart and more difficult on the guitar. Meanwhile, some chord voicings that are physically closer on guitar are farther apart and more difficult to play on the piano. Therefore, classic and established chord forms and voicings for the guitar are essential to the technique. Here are some more of these important chord forms for the diatonic 7th chords. Memorize these chords if you don't already know them.

(FIG. 4-11) Diatonic 7th Chord Forms

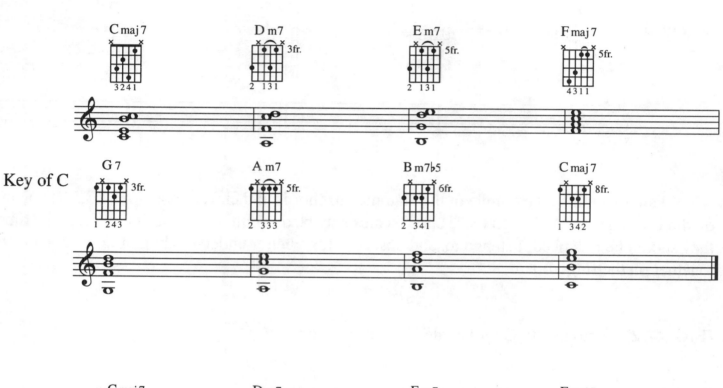

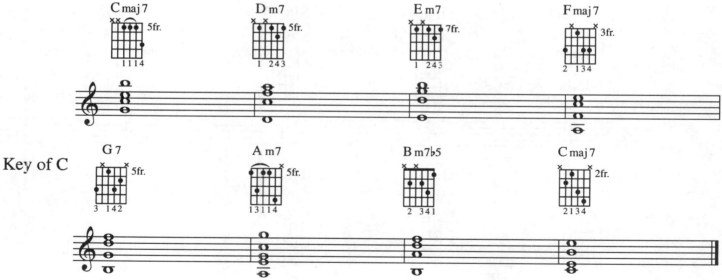

(FIG. 4-11) cont.

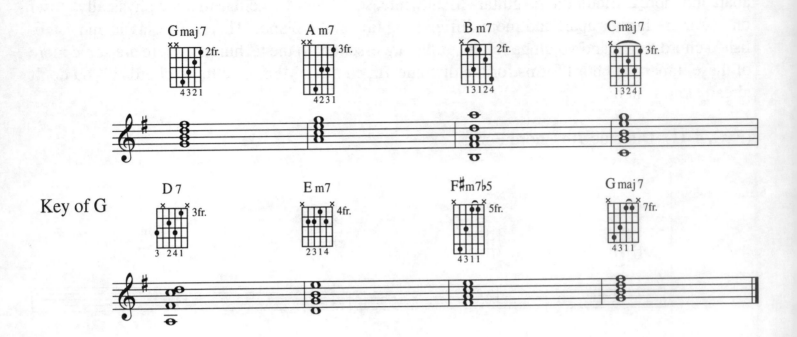

Key of G

I am including an example of the diatonic 7th chords in their root position (1,3,5,7) voicing on three string sets. Although these chord scales may be difficult to play at first or for some time, they should be practiced, listened to, and observed for a better understanding of how 3rds are put together on the fingerboard.

(FIG. 4-12) Diatonic 7th Chord Scale in Root Position

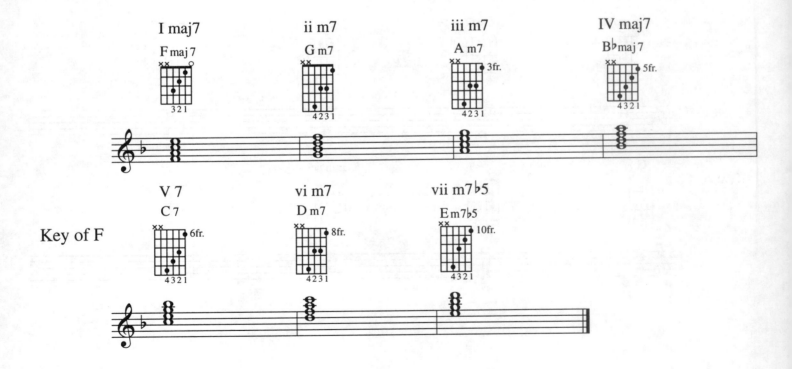

Key of F

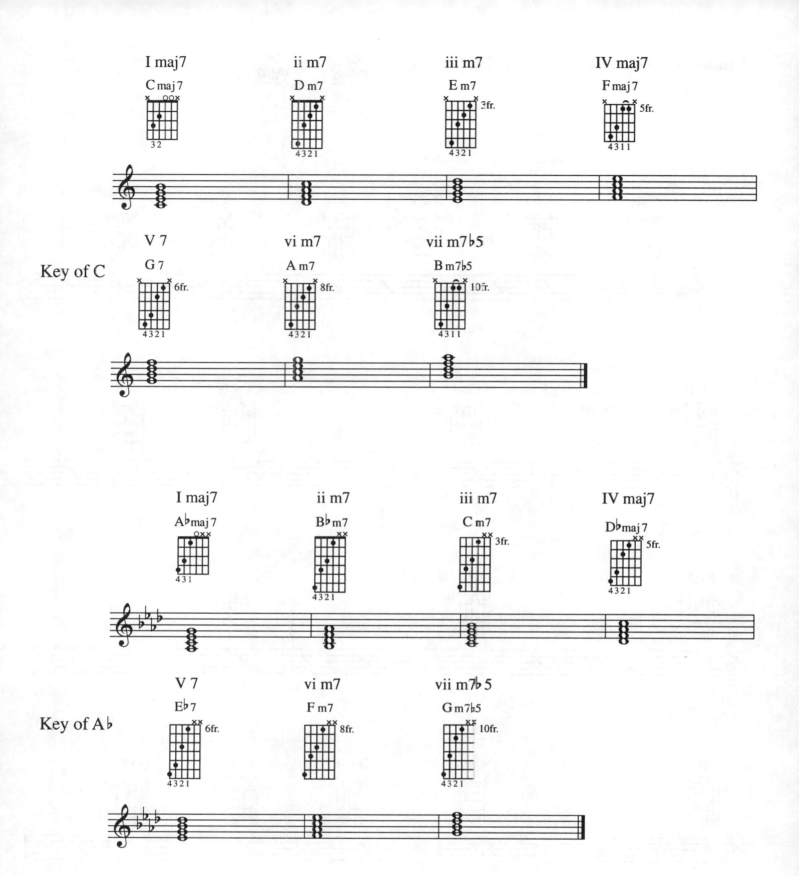

Transpose to the other twelve major keys.

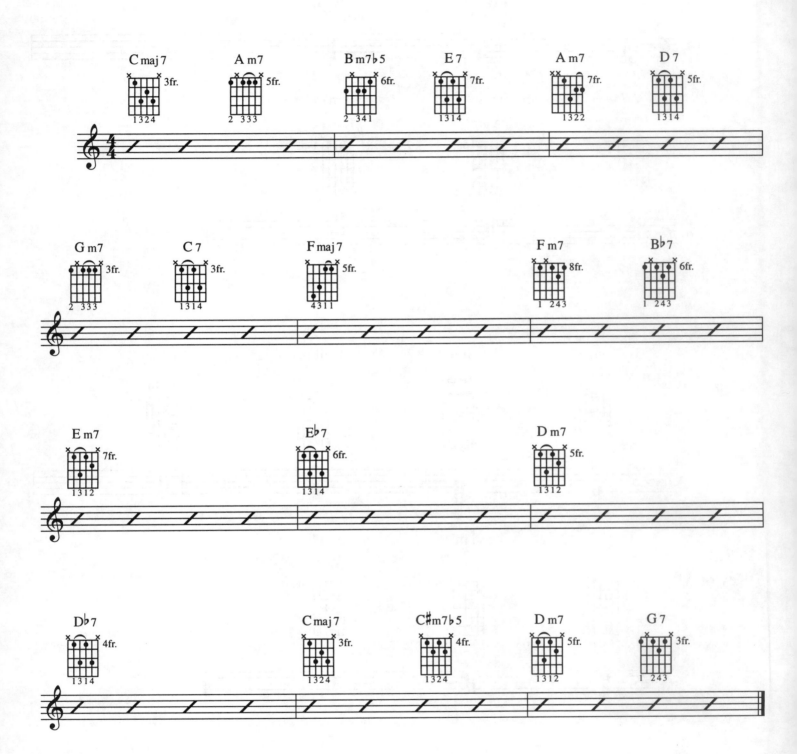

The Modes

Each of the seven degrees of the major scale has a mode which diatonically corresponds or belongs to the chord of that scale degree. Figure (4-13) shows the modes. Follow the fingering. Play the chord, then the corresponding mode, and familiarize yourself with the sound of it. Since the modes are one of the tools or elements of improvisation, it's important to hear and know them well, but remember - they are only one tool, and you can't build a house with only a hammer. They must be incorporated with many other elements for a well-rounded improvisational technique.

(FIG. 4-13) The Modes of the Major Scale (Key of C Major)

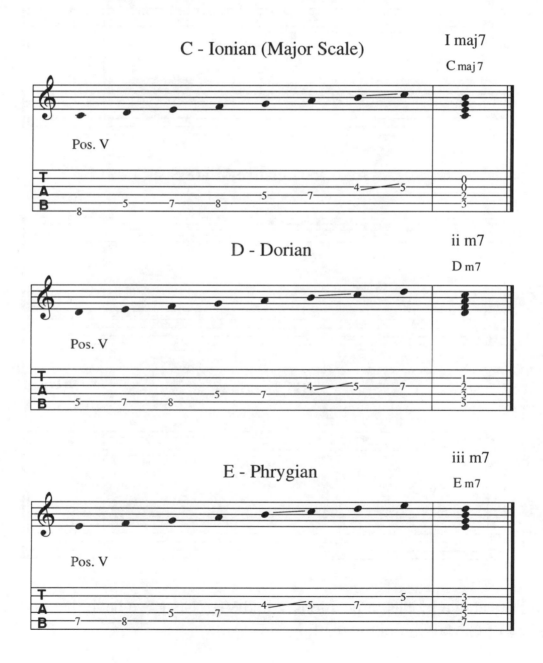

(FIG. 4-13) cont.

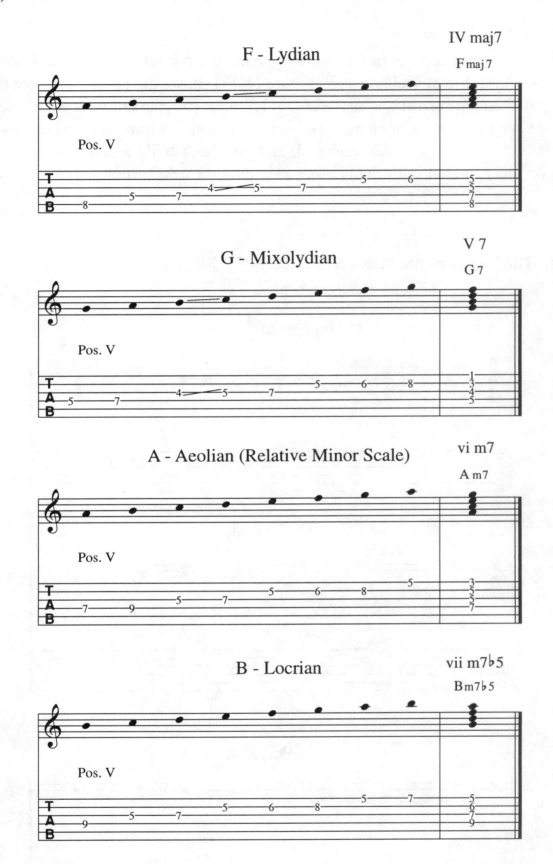

Play all the above modes in positions V and VII. Next, we have the modes (two octaves each) in the key of G Major. Follow the fingering.

(FIG. 4-14) The Modes of the Major Scale (Key of G Major)

G - Ionian (Major Scale)

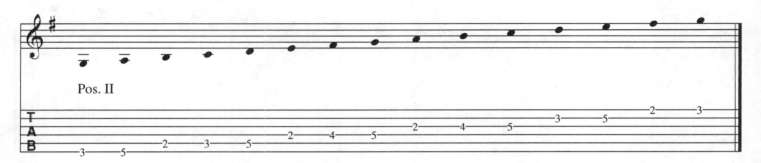

A - Dorian

B - Phrygian

C - Lydian

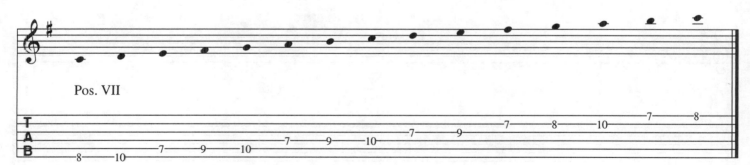

(FIG. 4-14) cont.

D - Mixolydian

E - Aeolian (Relative or Natural Minor)

F#- Locrian

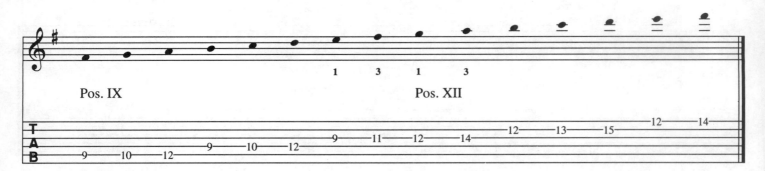

G - Ionian

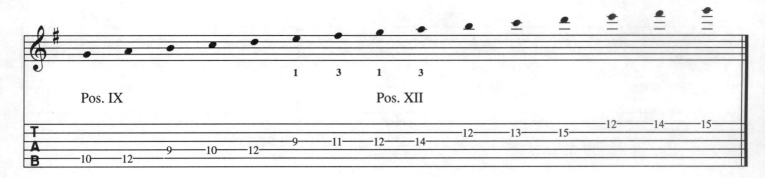

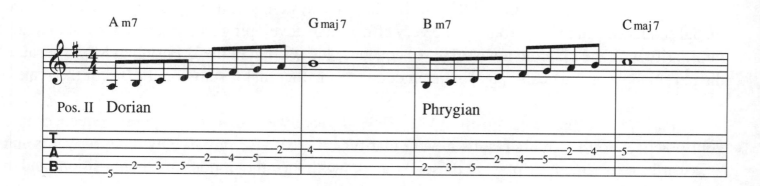

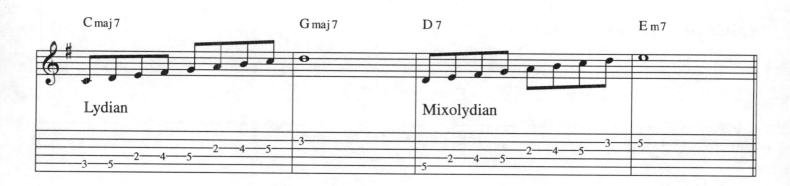

Sequences

A "sequence" is a group of intervals or notes that systematically repeats itself. Here are two modal sequences that I have found to be very effective in developing technique and in establishing familiarity with the diatonic notes. These sequences are written in the B Phrygian Mode because the phrygian has a musically pleasing sound, due to the fact that it starts on the 3rd of the scale.

Play both sequences in Position VII. Pick alternately and incorporate these sequences into your practice; you'll see big results in your clarity and speed. Be sure to play them forwards and backwards. Experiment by playing these sequences with the other modes in other positions and in other keys. Take your time.

(FIG. 4-15) B Phrygian Sequence

Sequence in Thirds

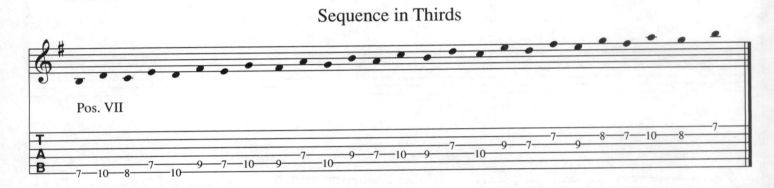

Four-note Sequence

46

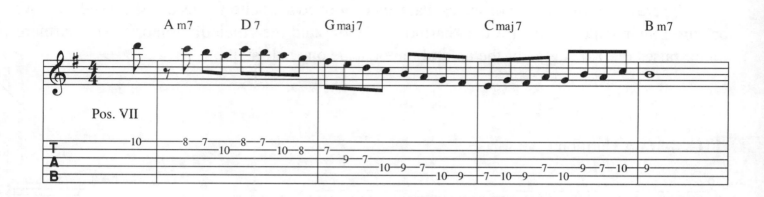

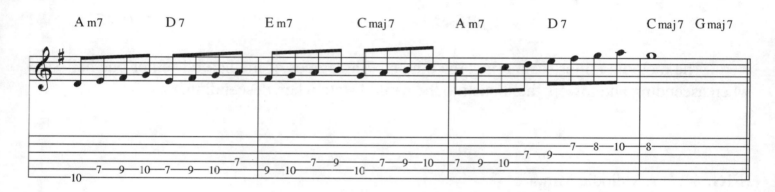

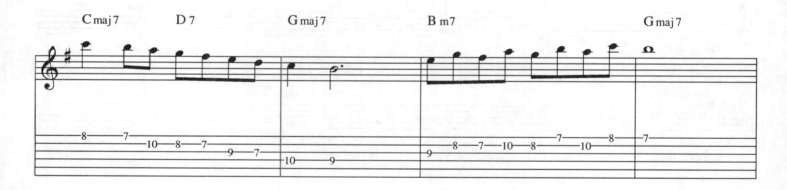

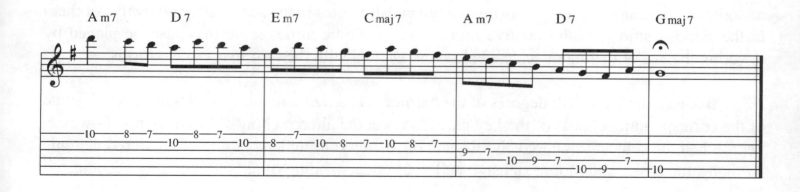

Harmonic and Melodic Minor Scales

There are two other minor scales that may be looked at as alterations of the natural (relative) or pure minor scale. They are the "harmonic minor" and the "melodic minor." The harmonic minor raises the 7th degree of the natural minor scale one half-step.

(FIG. 4-16) A Harmonic Minor

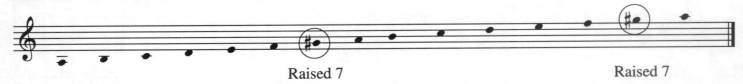

Raised 7   Raised 7

The melodic minor scale raises the 6th and 7th degrees of the natural minor one half-step when ascending and lowers them back to the natural state when descending.

(FIG. 4-17) A Melodic Minor

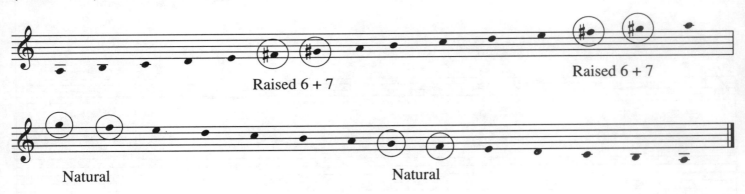

Raised 6 + 7   Raised 6 + 7

Natural   Natural

Take the four relative minor scale forms previously given and play them as harmonic and melodic minor scales simply by raising the 6th and 7th notes in the scale. Play all twelve of them in the same positions as the relative minor. The melodic minor scale may also be played by lowering the 3rd of the major scale a half-step. Do this with the four major scale forms.

Because the 6th or 7th degrees of the harmonic and melodic minor scales are altered, some of the corresponding chords of the key may also become altered chords. We have not, however, yet reached the subject of altered chords, and the better your understanding of unaltered diatonic harmony, the easier and more extensive will your understanding of altered harmony become.

The most common function of the harmonic minor scale is that it allows the V chord of the minor key to become a dominant chord as it is in the major key, by raising the minor 3rd to a major 3rd. (Ex. Em7 becomes E7 in the key of A minor)

The most common diatonic function of the melodic minor is that it defines the construction of a minor 6th chord with a major 6th by raising the 6th of the natural minor scale to a major 6th.

(Ex. A, C, E, F# = A minor 6)

Etude 8 - Harmonic, Melodic Minor

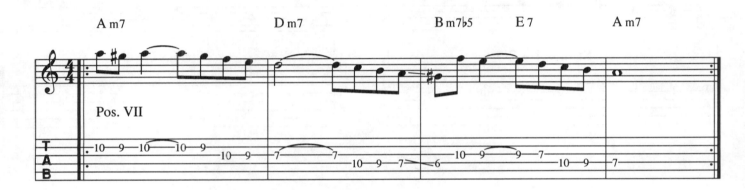

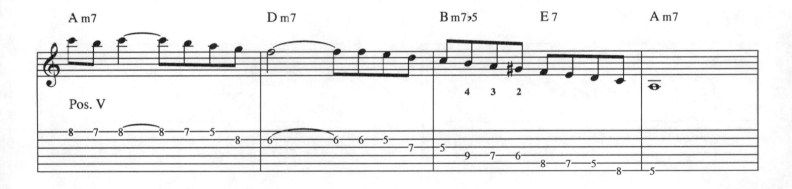

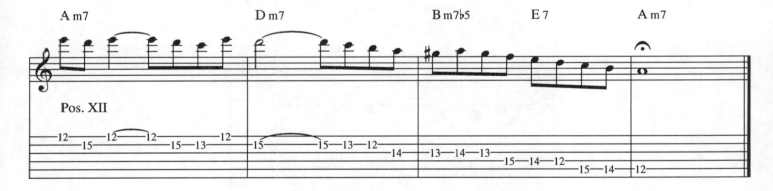

Before leaving the subject of 3rds, we want to be sure we are comfortable with the way they look, sound, and feel on the guitar, since they are so vital to key center harmony. The following shows how 3rds are played on each string set. The examples are in the key of C. Practice transposing 3rds to the other fourteen keys. (Ex. For the key of F, do the same thing, but flat all of the B notes)

(FIG. 4-18) Thirds on Each String Set (Key of C Major)

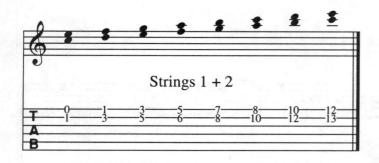

Strings 1 + 2

Strings 2 + 3

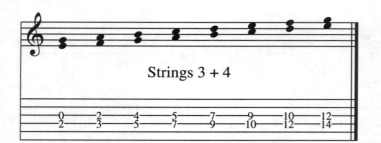

Strings 3 + 4

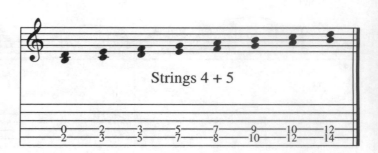

Strings 4 + 5

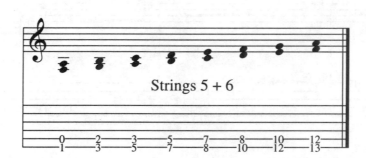

Strings 5 + 6

(FIG. 4-19) Inverted Thirds on Each String Set (Key of C Major)

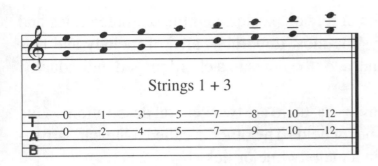

Strings 1 + 3

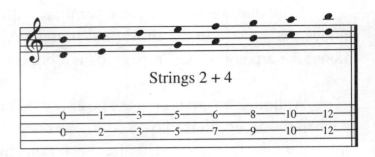

Strings 2 + 4

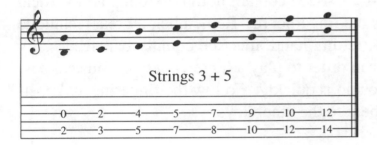

Strings 3 + 5

Strings 4 + 6

(FIG. 4-20) Key of F Major

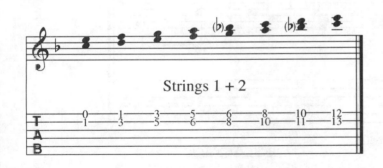

Strings 1 + 2

Continue on your own.

Arpeggios

Now that we have become familiar with the chromatic scales, and the diatonic scales and modes, let's move to the third (and in many ways the most important) area of melody and harmony: the arpeggio. An "arpeggio" is a broken chord, or the notes in a chord played individually.

Although an arpeggio may be executed many ways, there are two general descriptions. One is when the arpeggio is played while the chord is being held. The other is called a "linear" arpeggio, where the finger is lifted after each note, as in a melody line or lick (fig. 4-21).

Although you should practice the first type of arpeggio with chords and chord progressions, it is the second as linear type with which we are now concerned

The following arpeggios (fig. 4-22, 4-23, 4-24, 4-25) contain both horizontal and vertical fingerings, moving both up and down and across the fingerboard. Remember, a great technique requires that all four fingers of the left hand, or fretting hand, must be equally balanced. Any finger may be required to follow any other finger in order to play a large variety of musical passages. This means the ability to move through positions quickly. Follow the fingering and positions closely, learn the arpeggios and transpose them to the other keys.

(FIG. 4-21)

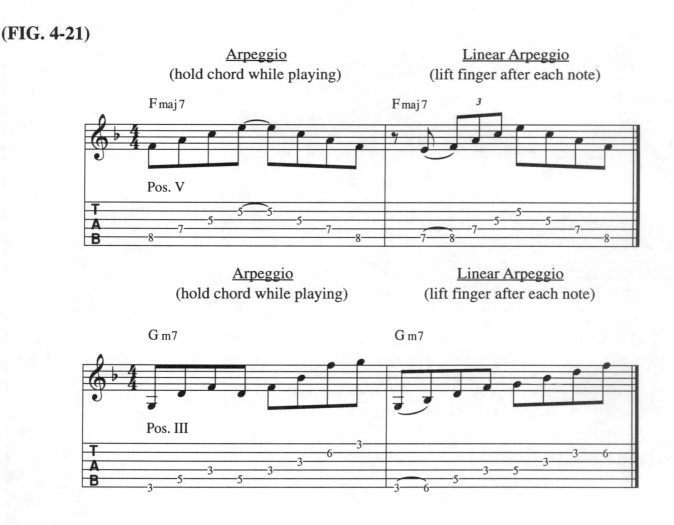

(FIG. 4-22) Diatonic 7th Chord Arpeggios (Key of G Major)

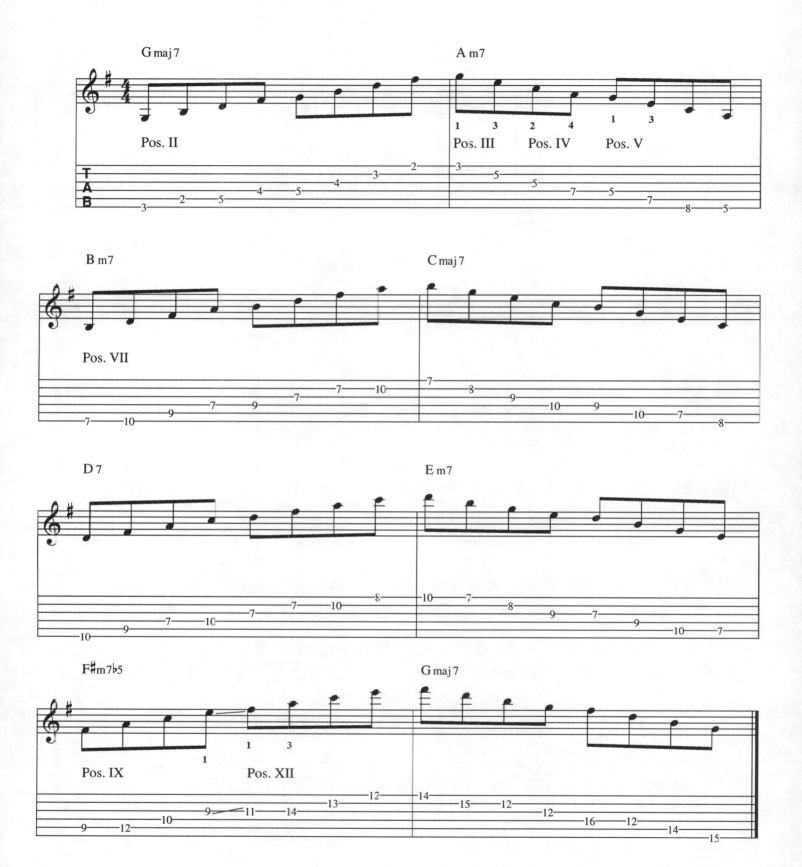

(FIG. 4-23) Diatonic 7th Chord Arpeggios (Key of C Major)

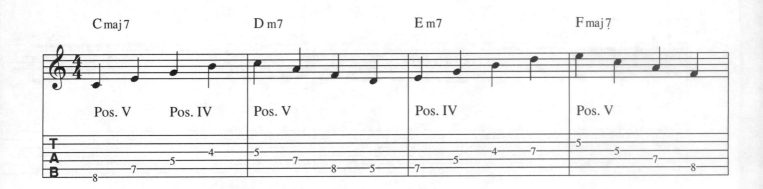

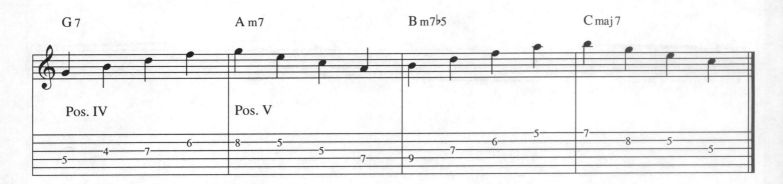

(FIG. 4-24) Diatonic 7th Chord Arpeggios (Key of G Major)

The next group of arpeggios (fig. 4-25) includes all of the essential fingerings and forms for the 7th chords. As you become familiar with these forms you may want to practice playing their inversions.

(FIG. 4-25) 7th Chord Arpeggio Forms

A maj 7

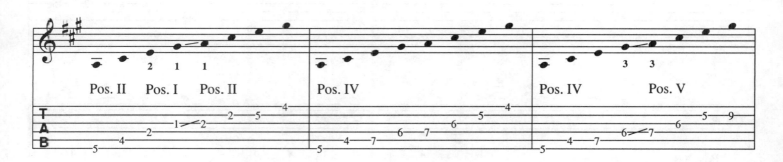

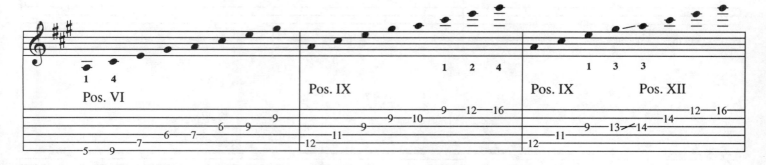

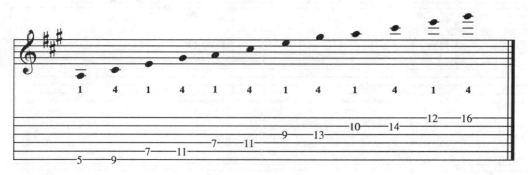

(FIG. 4-25) cont.

Am7

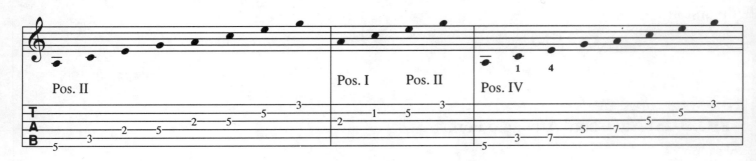

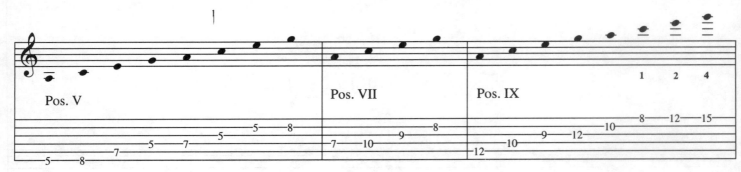

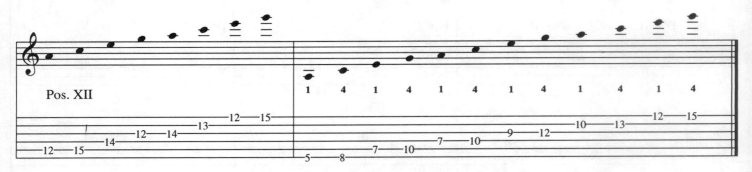

A7

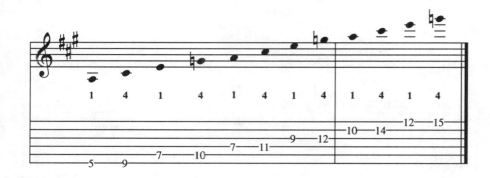

Am7♭5

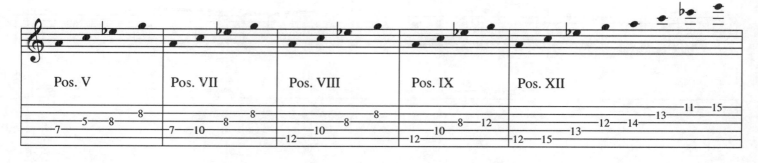

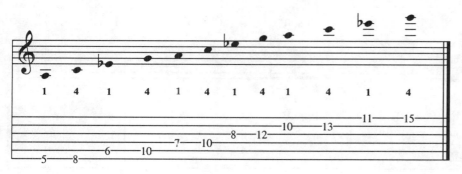

Etude 9 - Arpeggios in F Major

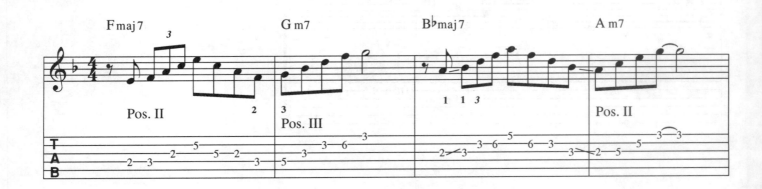

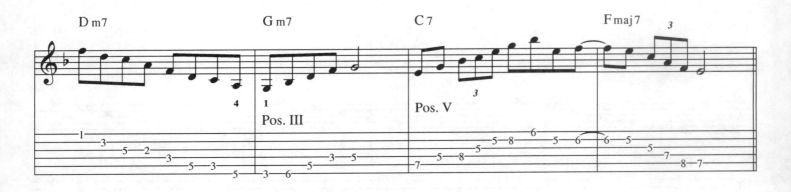

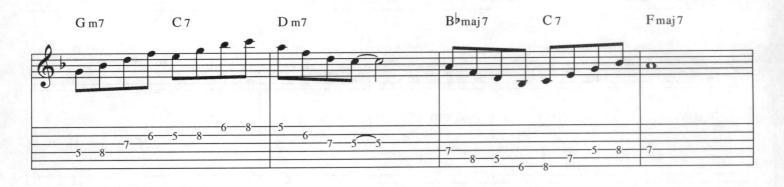

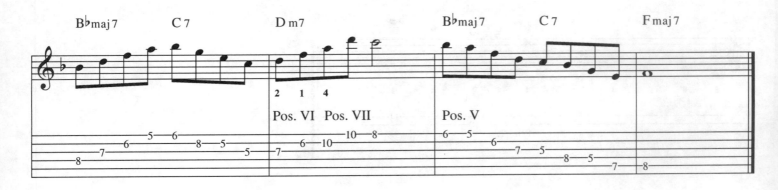

The Pentatonic Scale

The "pentatonic" scale is a five (penta) note (tonic) scale that is frequently used in jazz as well as many other styles of music. It is commonly called the "basic blues scale" because of its blues sound and extensive use in blues music. This is due to the fact that, in part, jazz evolved out of fundamental blues. There is a strong blues influence in a great deal of jazz. If you don't know them, the five inversions (or modes) of the pentatonic scale are a must in your repertoire of scales. Here they are.

(FIG. 4-26) Five Pentatonic Scale Forms

Form 1

Form 2

Form 3

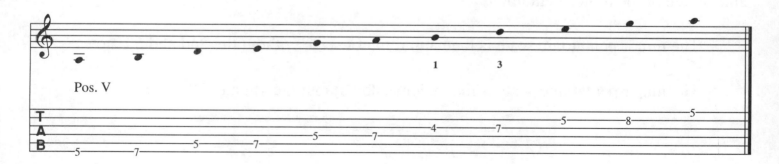

(FIG. 4-26) cont.

Form 4

Form 5

(Form 1 an octave higher, Pos. XII)

The minor pentatonic scale becomes the relative major pentatonic scale by starting on the 2nd degree of the minor Pentatonic.

The minor pentatonic scale is the natural minor scale without the 2nd and 6th notes.

The major pentatonic scale is the major scale without the 4th and 7th notes.

Etude 10 - Pentatonic Blues

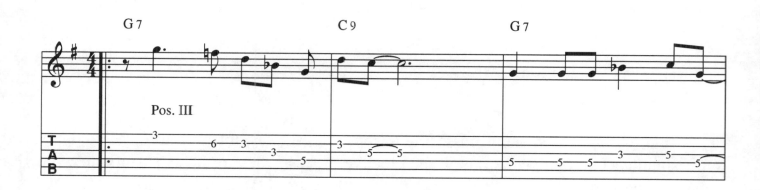

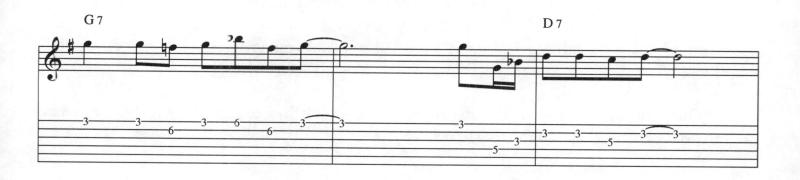

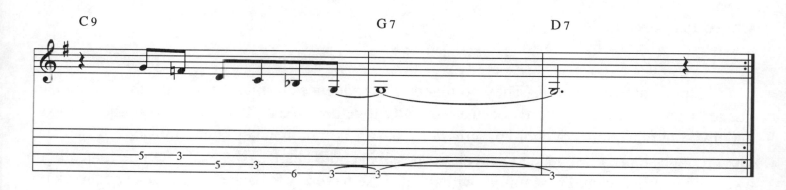

Chapter 5 – Improvising Over Chord Changes

Spontaneous Composition

Improvisation is spontaneous composition. It is the heartbeat of jazz. Mind, body, and spirit simultaneously move as one in the creative process. The result is an infinite variety of musical expression.

Spontaneous composition must, however, take place instantly in an immediate time frame because the music is in constant motion from start to finish, as opposed to "still" composition or writing music which, although it may be inspired, can be done in an indefinite period of time, ranging from one minute to ten years. All of your harmonic and compositional knowledge and technique must be immediately available for use and performance. Many times, the difference between a good player and a great player is that the great player can get to and use his or her knowledge faster than a good player can.

Melody, harmony, and rhythm must come together at once in improvisation with feeling and interpretation. It's like riding a roller coaster or ferris wheel (which is why taking a solo is often called "taking a ride"). It's like flying and gives you a sense of freedom. That's what is great about jazz. It takes a lot of practice, but it's a lot of fun, and you never stop getting better unless you want to.

Now let's start putting together chromaticism, scales, modes, and arpeggios over chord progressions and songs as we move into deeper waters.

Chord Progressions

Chords are like words. They go together in sequences to make musical sense in the language of music. Certain chords occur frequently together, like certain words, and one learns to anticipate certain chords or chord progressions that are common in key center music. Let's look at these progressions. First, let's look at all the possible chord changes that can occur diatonically in a key and play, learn, and get familiar with them. Listen closely to each chord change and work on remembering what they sound like so you can begin to recognize them when you hear them being played.

(FIG. 5-1) The Diatonic Chord Changes

These are two-chord, two-bar progressions. Play the progressions forward and backward.

I maj7	ii m7	I maj7	iii m7	I maj7	IV maj7
C maj7	D m7	C maj7	E m7	C maj7	F maj7

I maj7	V 7	I maj7	vi m7	I maj7	vii m7♭5
C maj7	G 7	C maj7	A m7	C maj7	B m7♭5

ii m7	I maj7	ii m7	iii m7	ii m7	IV maj7
D m7	C maj7	D m7	E m7	D m7	F maj7

ii m7	V 7	ii m7	vi m7	ii m7	vii m7♭5
D m7	G 7	D m7	A m7	D m7	B m7♭5

iii m7	I maj7	iii m7	ii m7	iii m7	IV maj7
E m7	C maj7	E m7	D m7	E m7	F maj7

iii m7	V 7	iii m7	vi m7	iii m7	vii m7♭5
E m7	G 7	E m7	A m7	E m7	B m7♭5

(FIG. 5-1) cont.

IV maj7	I maj7	IV maj7	ii m7	IV maj7	iii m7
Fmaj7	Cmaj7	Fmaj7	Dm7	Fmaj7	Em7

IV maj7	V 7	IV maj7	vi m7	IV maj7	vii m7♭5
Fmaj7	G7	Fmaj7	Am7	Fmaj7	Bm7♭5

V 7	I maj7	V 7	ii m7	V 7	iii m7
G7	Cmaj7	G7	Dm7	G7	Em7

V 7	IV maj7	V 7	vi m7	V 7	vii m7♭5
G7	Fmaj7	G7	Am7	G7	Bm7♭5

vi m7	I maj7	vi m7	ii m7	vi m7	iii m7
Am7	Cmaj7	Am7	Dm7	Am7	Em7

vi m7	IV maj7	vi m7	V 7	vi m7	vii m7♭5
Am7	Fmaj7	Am7	G7	Am7	Bm7♭5

vii m7♭5	I maj7	vii m7♭5	ii m7	vii m7♭5	iii m7
Bm7♭5	Cmaj7	Bm7♭5	Dm7	Bm7♭5	Em7

vii m7♭5	IV maj7	vii m7♭5	V 7	vii m7♭5	vi m7
Bm7♭5	Fmaj7	Bm7♭5	G7	Bm7♭5	Am7

The Perfect 4th

The next-higher interval after the major 3rd is the "perfect 4th;" two-and-a-half steps or five frets on the guitar. This interval, along with the third, is probably the most important in jazz or even tonal music. Although chords are built with 3rds, the natural movement of chords and keys is with 4ths. When the twelve notes are written a fourth apart, they become what is commonly called "the cycle of 4ths."

(FIG. 5-2) The Cycle of Fourths

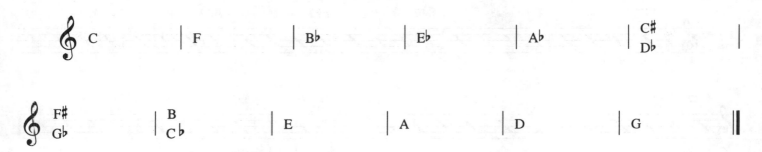

Because the most important chord progressions move in 4ths, and because the transposition of keys (due to the number of accidentals) also moves in 4ths, this cycle is a common denominator in jazz and should be known and memorized backward and forward. Most things learned in all keys should be done moving through the cycle of 4ths because it is the natural order of resolution (and most things should be learned in all fifteen keys).

In his live set, Gene Ammons (Jug) used to play a twelve-bar blues in every key, moving through the cycle of 4ths. This is a great way to really learn a tune.

Chord Progressions in Fourths

The most important and common chord progressions in jazz move in 4ths.

Ex.	I maj7	to	IV 7		C maj7	to	F maj7
	ii m7	to	V 7		D m7	to	G 7
	V7	to	I maj7		G7	to	C maj7
	vi m7	to	ii m7		A m7	to	D m7
	iii m7	to	vi m7		E m7	to	A m7

The following three figures (5-3, 5-4, 5-5) show the three most important cycle of 4ths progressions. Practice and memorize them, and you'll be well on the way to uderstanding jazz chord progressions and resolutions.

(FIG. 5-3) Dominant 7th Cycle of Fourths Progression

Ex. 1

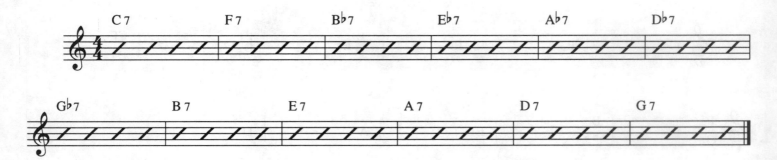

Ex. 2

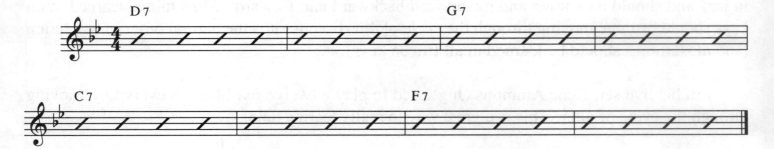

Ex. 3

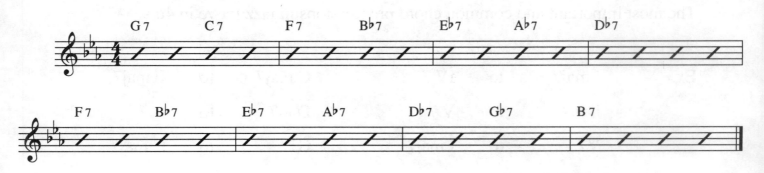

Etude 11 - Playing Through the Dominant 7th Cycle of Fourths Progression

Probably the most important two-chord progression in jazz is shown in figure (5-4). Notice how every 3rd chord becomes the ii m7 chord in the next key instead of the I maj7 which would be the expected chord of resolution.

(FIG. 5-4) Cycle of Fourths Moving in the ii m7 V 7 Progression

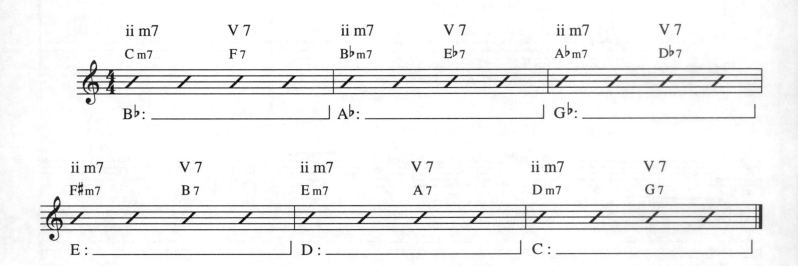

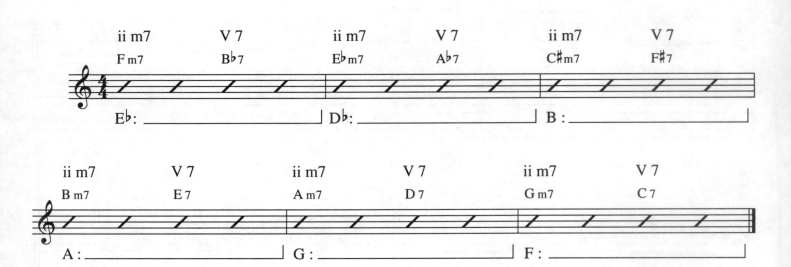

Figure (5-5) shows the most important three-chord progression in jazz moving through the cycle of fourths.

(FIG. 5-5) Cycle of Fourths Moving in the ii m7 V 7 I maj7 Progression

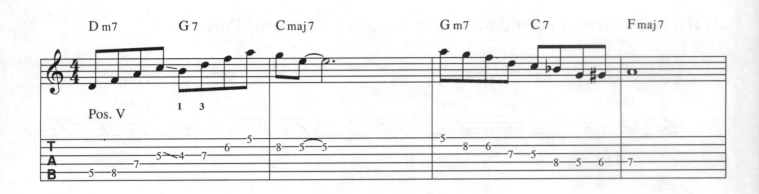

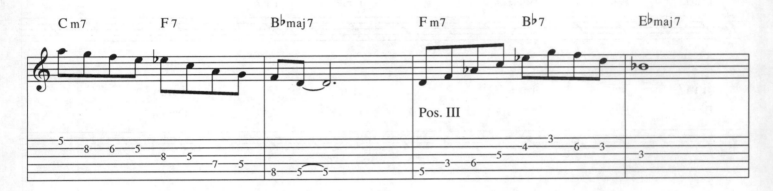

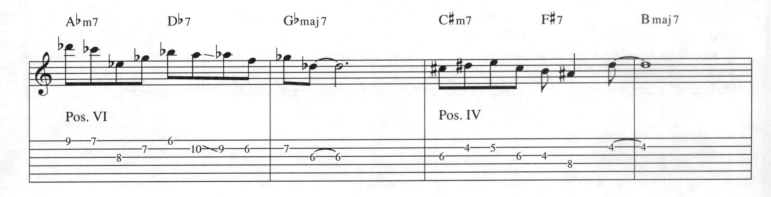

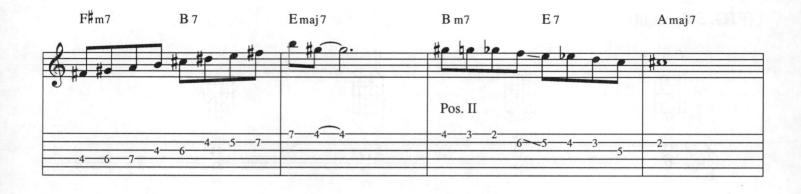

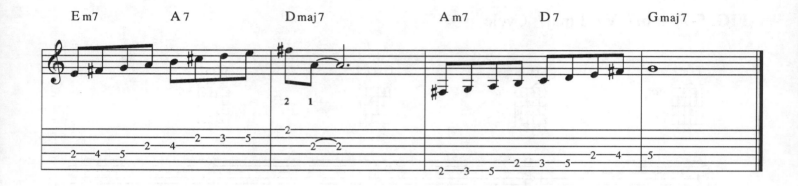

Figure (5-6) shows six sets of ii m7 V 7 chords. Learn them, play the ii m7 V 7 cycle of fourths progression shown in figure (5-4) using only the first four chords, then practice the cycle using all six sets of chords.

(FIG. 5-6) Six Sets of ii m7 V7 Chords

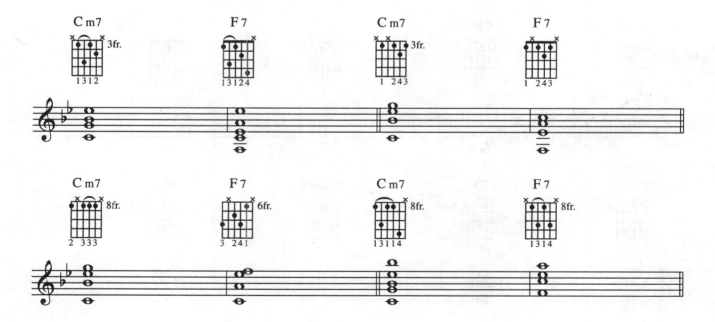

(FIG. 5-6) cont.

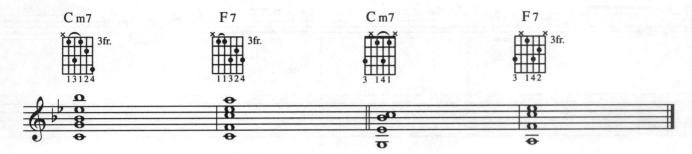

(FIG. 5-7) ii m7 V7 I maj7 Cycle

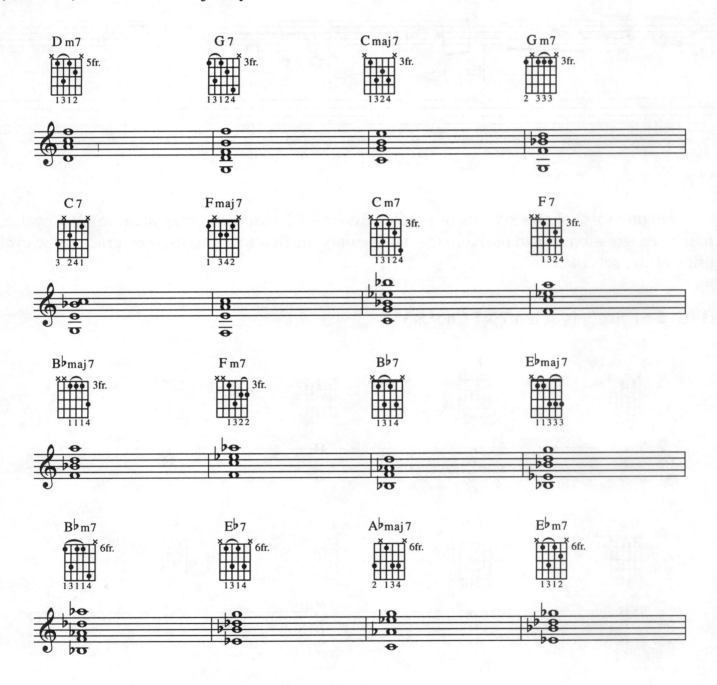

The Remaining Intervals

Augmented 4th	=	3 whole steps or 6 frets
Diminished 5th	=	3 whole steps or 6 frets
Perfect 5th	=	3-1/2 steps or 7 frets
Augmented 5th	=	4 whole steps or 8 frets
Minor 6th	=	4 whole steps or 8 frets
Major 6th	=	4-1/2 steps or 9 frets
Minor 7th	=	5 whole steps or 10 frets
Major 7th	=	5-1/2 steps or 11 frets
Octave	=	6 whole steps or 12 frets

The Turnaround

The most important four-chord progression in jazz is the I maj7, vi m7, ii m7, V7; commonly called a "turnaround." When we add a vi m7 chord to a ii m7, V 7, I maj7 and start the progression with the I maj7 chord, we have a turnaround. As well as being an important part of the harmony of many songs, it is also used to connect sections of songs. The turnaround should be thoroughly learned in all keys. It also has within its framework many important two-chord progressions.

Ex.	I maj7	to	vi m7
	vi m7	to	ii m7
	ii m7	to	V 7
	V7	to	I maj7
	I maj7	to	ii m7
	Imaj7	to	V 7

The I maj7 vi m7 ii m7 V 7 chord progression and its variations are shown in figure (5-8).

(FIG. 5-8)

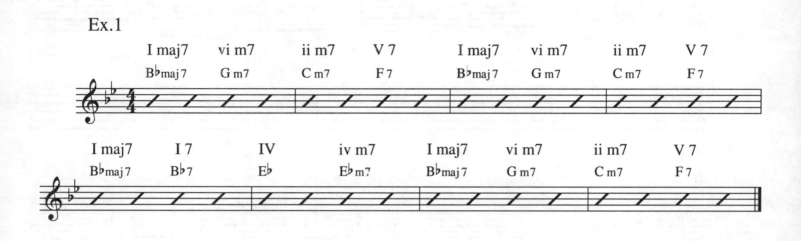

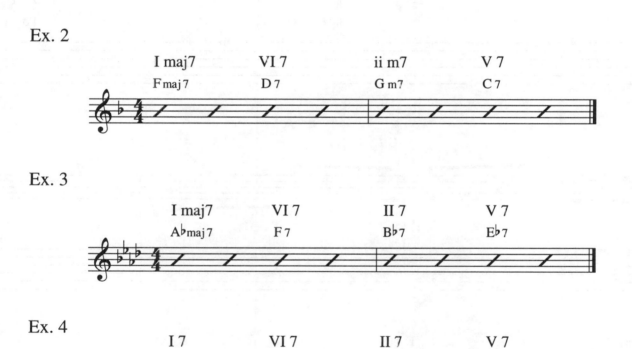

Example 1 shows the first eight measures of "Rhythm Changes", one of the most played chord progressions in jazz. Notice how it is almost entirely comprised of the I maj7 vi m7 ii m7 V 7 progression.

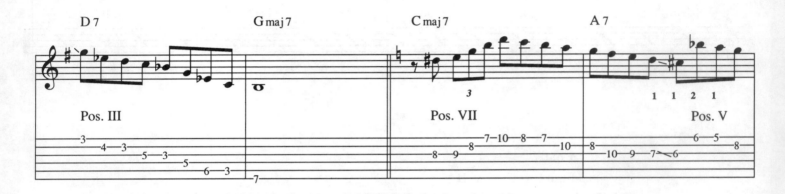

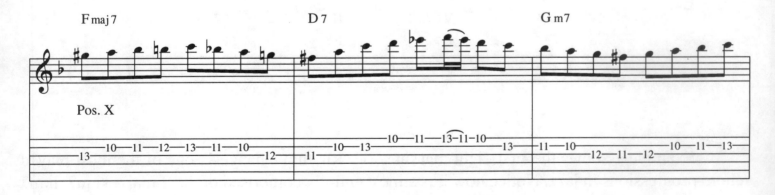

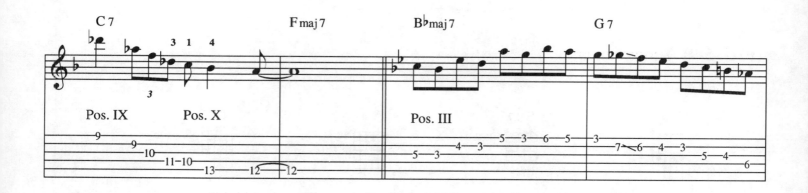

Figure (5-9) shows the I maj7 vi m7 ii m7 V 7 chord progression. Practice using chords we've already learned to create other voice leading combinations.

(FIG. 5-9) Turnarounds

Comping

"Comping" is a term used for the technique of accompaniment in jazz. This, of course, is a major part of your over-all playing technique. It is as important as your ability to play melody and solo.

There are two basic divisions of comping. The first is what I call "fixed" comping. It is a specific rhythmic pattern that remains consistent throughout the song or part but may have some variations. The second is "free-form" comping, which is improvised with no fixed patterns and in which themes or phrases are created. The two styles of comping may be combined.

Let's look at these two styles of comping.

Etude 14-A1 (FIG. 5-10) Fixed Comping Styles

Early jazz guitar swing. Feel the heavy down beat on 2 and 4.
(In the style of Django Reinhardt)

Early jazz guitar swing. Straight 4/4, short down beats, all even.
(In the style of Charlie Christian)

Etude 14-A2

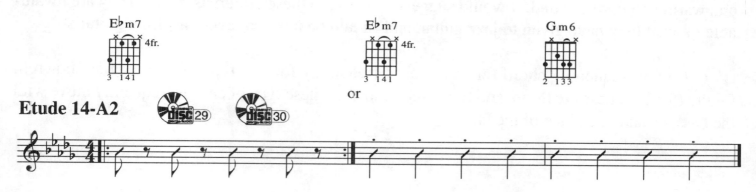

(FIG. 5-10) cont.

Etude 14-A3

Early jazz swing. Straight 4/4, with short beats on 2 and 4. (In the style of Les Paul)

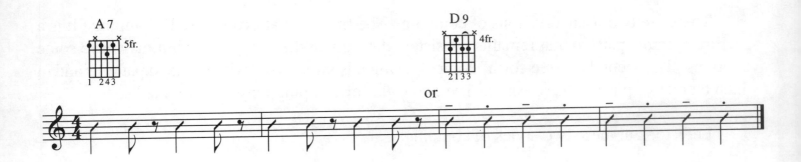

Typical Freddie Green rhythm; 4/4 early jazz swing with heavy attacks, low volume. Percussive, heavy accent on 2 and 4, sometimes 1 and 3.

Etude 14-A4

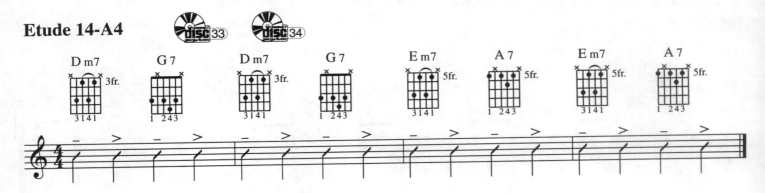

The comping styles of early jazz are best exemplified by the pioneers of early jazz guitar, the greats that have influenced all jazz guitarists since: Charlie Christian, Django Reinhardt, Les Paul, Freddie Green. This style of comping is best done with a low volume, full body, and crisp and warm percussive sound. I would suggest listening to these guitarists often. They are invaluable in what they have given to jazz guitar, and should be a part of every aspiring guitarist.

Certain sequential chord forms are used frequently for this type of comping as shown in Figure (5-11). These are three- and four-voice chords. These type of chords frequently move with the bass, or take the place of the bass.

(FIG. 5-11)

Three Voice Chords

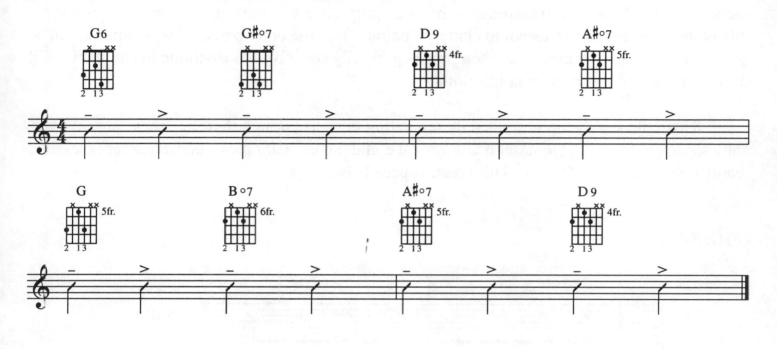

Four Voice Chords

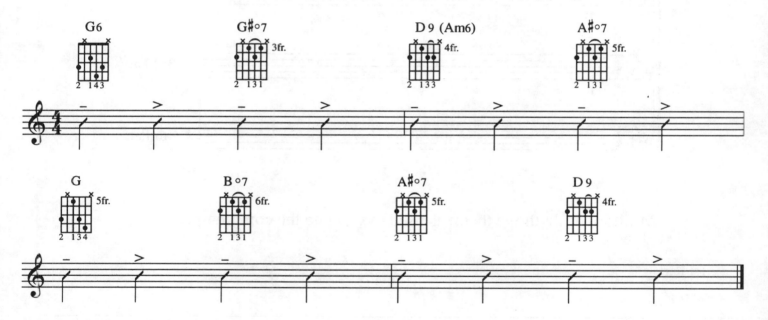

Let's turn our attention now to free-form comping, which is primarily improvisational. Lots of familiarity with chord progressions, sequences, and chord forms is essential in this type of comping, as you need this knowledge and execution at your immediate disposal to be creative and accurate. Let's look at some important elements of free-form comping.

1. Separation of Parts

Since the basic purpose of comping is to enhance, compliment, and contribute to the others' parts, be they solo or accompaniment, it becomes important that the comping be heard as a separate or independent part so as not to clutter or detract from the other parts. This separation can be achieved a number of ways. Since comping is primarily conceived as rhythmic in nature, we will deal with rhythmic separation at this point.

Rhythmic separation is created by separating the part through rhythm. These are rhythmically separated by playing quarter notes against eighth notes, half notes against quarter notes, and whole notes against half notes. This creates space between parts.

(FIG. 5-12)

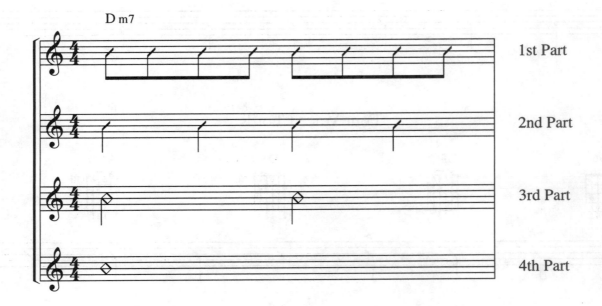

A different rhythmic theme is used to separate the comping part.

2. Spacing

Spacing of a comping part is effective in that it creates separation and gives the comping part a life of its own. Listening to the soloist or other parts is very important in choosing where to leave space and requires a lot of practice. Independence of the comping part should be sought so that the part is complete unto itself and has its own identity. By that I mean that if the comping part were played by itself, it would stand as a separate part and be definitive. This allows the part to be heard without interfering with the soloist or other parts. See Figure (5-13).

(FIG. 5-13)

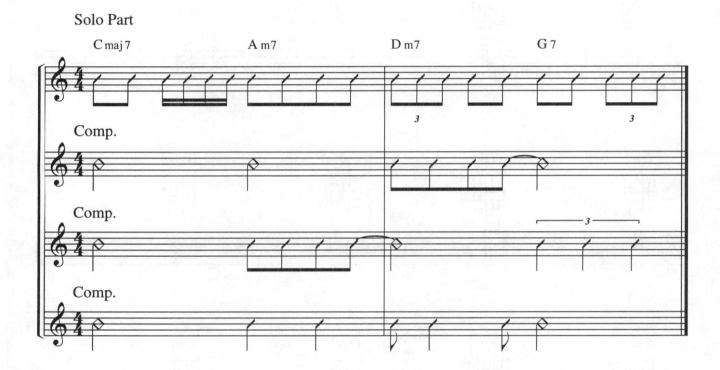

3. Melodic Themes

Short melodic themes also add to the definition of the comping part. This takes a lot of experimentation and practice. A whole volume could be covered on thematic development in this area. Be sure to keep the melody note (highest note in the chord) on top. Practice playing the chords as half notes so as to hear what is going on melodically as well as harmonically, and then practice playing the chords with different rhythms. This will really help you to hear chord tones as melody notes. Figure (5-14) shows a series of variations over a I maj7 IV 7 ii m7 V 7 chord progression

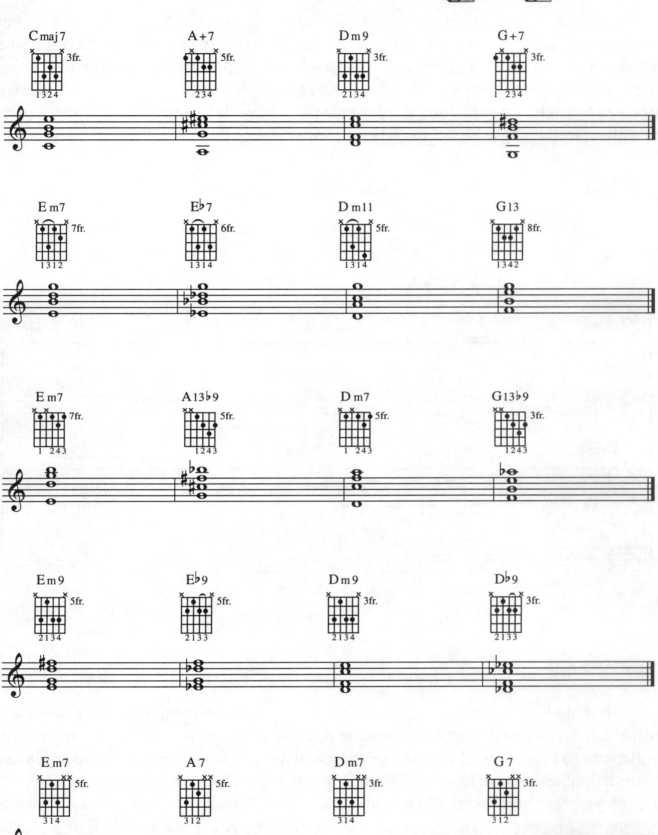

Before leaving the comping chapter, I have listed some examples of Latin rhythms in Figure (5-15). I urge you to practice and expand on these comping techniques.

Etude 14-C1 (FIG. 5-15)

Bossa Nova

Samba **14-C2**

Samba **14-C3**

Bolero **14-C4**

Chapter 6 – Solo Lines Over Chord Changes

Anticipation

One of the most important things in jazz improvisation is to develop the ability to anticipate chord changes. Music is in motion; playing is like driving a car. We must project ourselves *ahead* of where we are, while at the same time *being aware* of where we are. When a person is first learning to improvise, they frequently wait for the chord to change before playing anything. The idea is to look for the next chord before it gets there, so that we can direct the identity of what we are playing. This is called " identity direction."

Resolution

To play one chord into another, we must be able to resolve the chord into the next chord, so we must know where the "points of resolution" are, or the resolving notes of the next chord. The resolving points of a chord are the notes that are in that chord. The primary resolving notes are 1, 3, 5, and 7.

Let's look at some examples of resolution with the use of modes, arpeggios, and chromaticisms.

(FIG. 6-1)

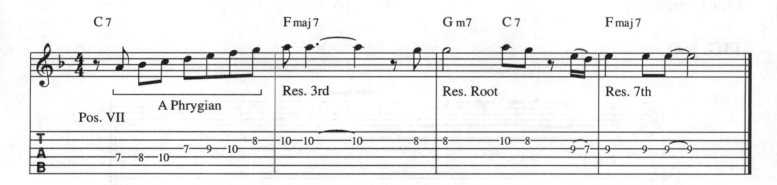

This example shows an A Phrygian mode over a C7 chord resolving to the 3rd of Fmaj7, moving to the root of Gm7, moving to the 7th of Fmaj7.

(FIG. 6-2)

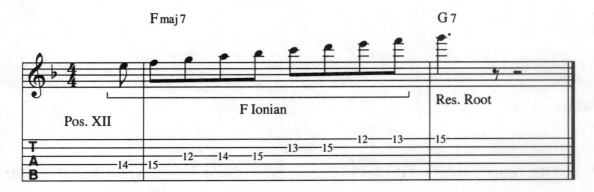

In this example, the F Ionian mode or major scale is used to move from an Fmaj7 to the root of G7 chord.

This next example uses an A Mixolydian mode to move from an A 9 to a Dmaj7 chord.

(FIG. 6-3)

A mode can be played from any of the chord tones in the chord for which you are using the mode. For example, this passage uses the mode from the 3rd of D minor, which is F Ionian, using it for D minor 7.

(FIG. 6-4)

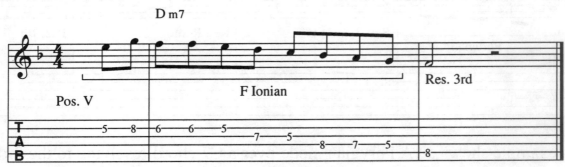

Use these lines as examples of mode, chromatic, and arpeggio combinations. Learn them well and listen to the chord progression and resolution within the line. Then, practice by creating your own combinations against diatonic chord progressions. Continue to practice the chromatic scales, diatonic scales, and arpeggios, because familiarity will allow you to be more creative.

Etude 15-A (FIG. 6-5) A ii m7, V7, I maj7 Progression in F

Etude 15-B (FIG. 6-6) A IV maj7, V7 Progression in B♭

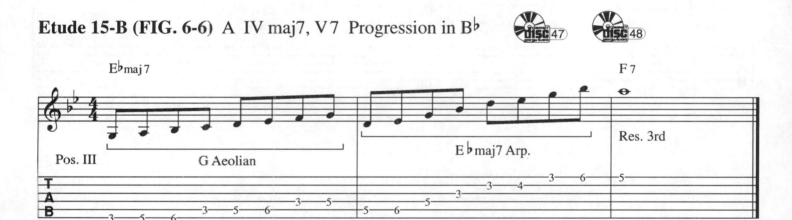

Etude 15-C (FIG. 6-7) A IV maj7, iii m7, ii m7 Progression in E♭

Etude 15-D (FIG. 6-8) A ii m7, V 7, I maj7 Progression in G

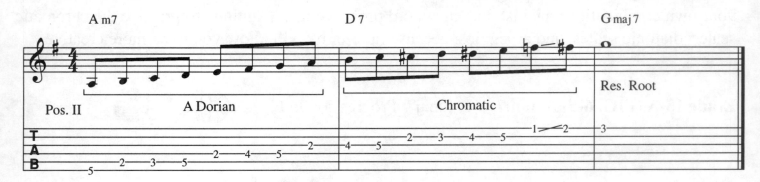

Etude 15-E (FIG. 6-9) A ii m7, iii m7, ii m7 Progression in A

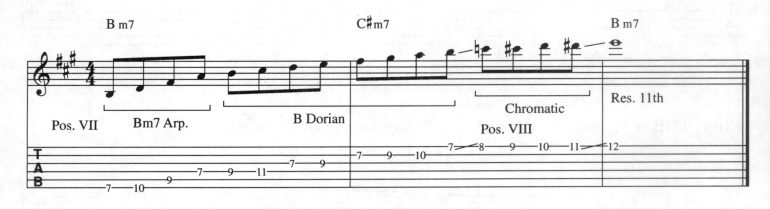

Chapter 7 – Developing Staccato (Picking) and Legato (Slurring) Techniques

Attaining a good technique requires the synchronization or balancing of both hands working together.

Legato

"Legato" is a musical term that means smooth or connected. Any means of producing a smooth or connected sound of notes is called a legato technique. Every instrument has its own legato techniques. Legato techniques on the guitar are: slurs (hammer-ons and pull-offs), slides, sweeps, and rakes, or any combination of the above.

Staccato

"Staccato" is a musical term that means broken or separated. Any means of producing separately sounding notes is labeled a staccato technique. A general meaning of staccato on the guitar would be picked notes, or notes that are picked separately.

Having a good playing technique calls for equally developed legato and staccato technique. In other words, you have to be able to pick and slur equally well. Many times, with a fairly developed player, the picking technique is not as fast as the slurring or legato technique.

The following is the best legato and picking combination exercise that I have found. When executed correctly, every day, it will double the quality of your overall technique in one or two weeks. It will balance both hands really well because you are picking two notes and slurring two notes alternately throughout the entire exercise at the same speed, using eighth or sixteenth notes. Be sure to observe the following points when you learn and practice this exercise.

1. Play all notes evenly

2. Play at a slow tempo at first, until you have control.

3. Try to make both picked and slurred notes dynamically the same.

4. Be sure you are following the up- and down-strokes of the pick correctly.

5. Once you know the exercise, start at the 12th position, play the entire exercise once, then move down to the 11th position. Continue moving chromatically down the neck through the 1st position. Play the exercise without stopping between positions.

You may have to stop when your arm starts to tighten or cramp (usually around the 7th or 6th position). The trick is to stop for a short period of time only (maybe one minute or ninety seconds), then continue down to the end of the neck without stopping. Doing this exercise even once a day is equal to practicing an hour.

Etude 16 - Legato Study

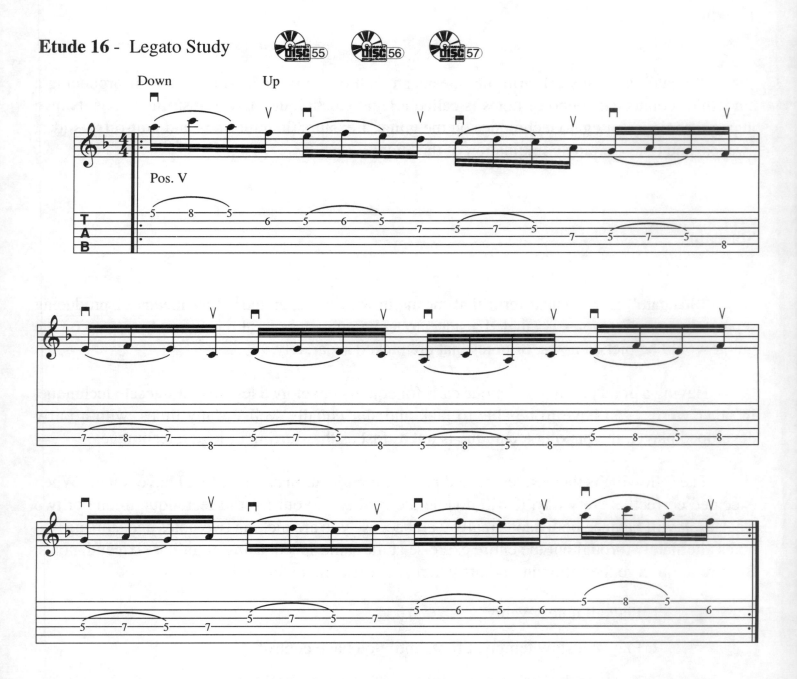

All notes are the same speed. The two picked notes must be the same speed as the two slurred notes.

Chapter 8 – Identifying Chromaticism

Chromaticism in a non-tonal technique of composition insomuch as it has no key center identity or harmonic identity of its own. It is used, and has been used for centuries, to create some of the most beautiful and musical lines and melodies in music. Chromaticism, being a harmonic non-entity, can be given harmonic identity in a number of ways. A chromatic line may be harmonically identified, for example, by breaking it with chord tones and then continuing it. A chromatic line may also be followed by a diatonic passage. Below are some examples of both.

This process creates some great improvisational lines and colors. You can create your own once you become familiar with the technique.

Etude 17-A (FIG. 8-1) - Chromatic Lines Identified by Chord Tones and Diatonic Passages

Ex. 1 Play for D Minor, F Major, or G 7

Etude 17-B

Ex. 2 Play for D Minor, F Major, or G 7

Etude 17-C Ex. 3 Play for C Major, A Minor, or D 7

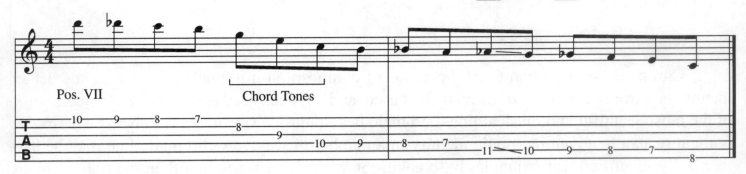

Etude 17-D Ex. 4 Play for B♭ Major, G Minor, or C 7

Etude 17-E Ex. 5 Play for C °7

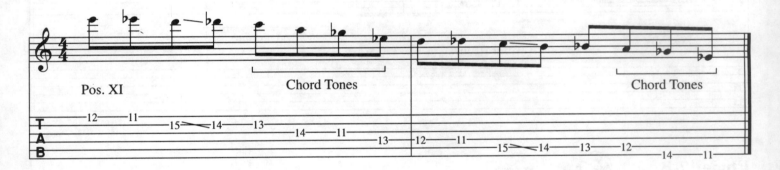

Etude 17-F Ex. 6 Play for G7♯5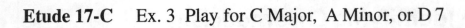

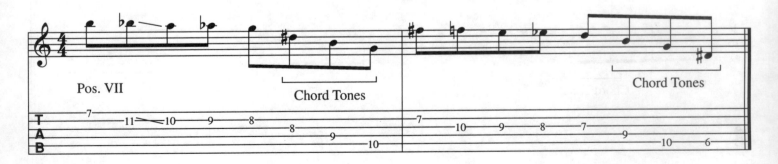

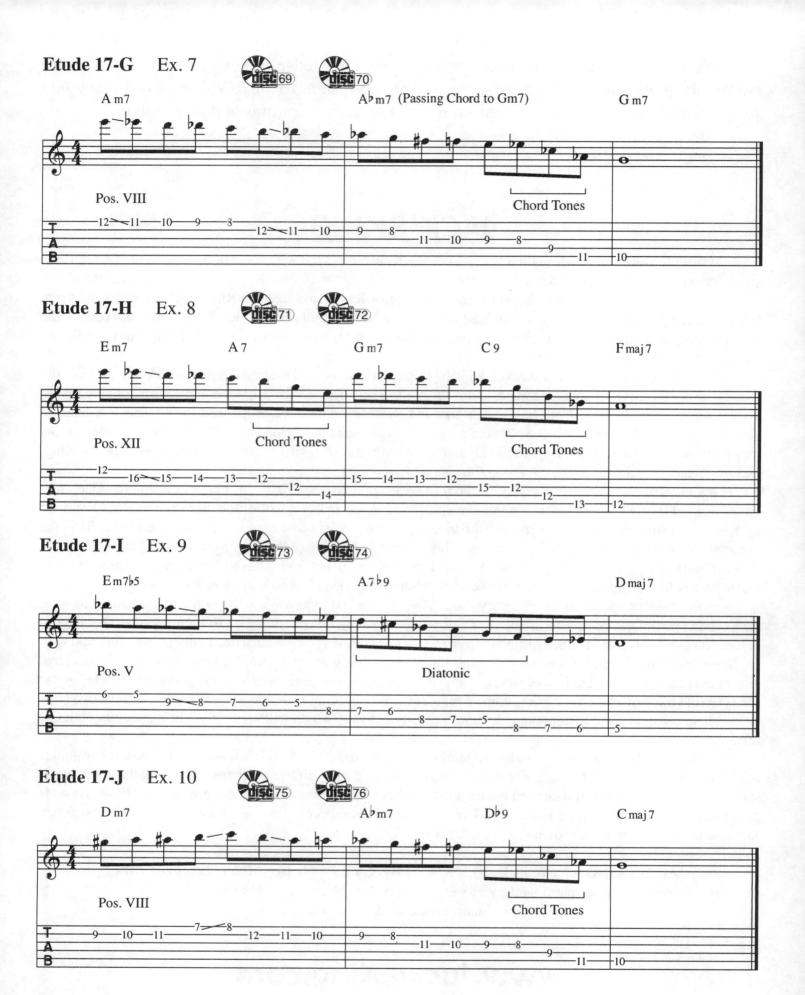

Now that you have a good understanding and knowledge of key centered music, scales, modes, arpeggios, and chord progressions, you are ready to move on to Volume 2 of *Getting Into Jazz*, which covers more advanced material and short-cuts to learning and performing.

Good luck! *Jackie King*

JACKIE KING

Over the past four decades guitar virtuoso Jackie King has played with some of America's greatest musical artists, providing sterling accompaniment on various occasions for the likes of Ray Charles, Tony Bennett and Big Joe Turner, and matching his six-string skills on stage against Jerry Garcia, Stevie Ray Vaughn and Eric Johnson. But where King has really earned his sizable reputation as a brilliant and fleet-fingered improviser has been in the realm of jazz, and since the early 1970s, he has spent most of his time working with legends like Chet Baker, Sonny Stitt and Jimmy Witherspoon.

For nearly two years now, however, King has been performing and touring steadily with Willie Nelson, the greatly-loved maverick of country music, and if this partnership seems somewhat incongruous it actually makes perfect sense when one considers how much jazz and western swing have influenced their respective musical developments. While many of Nelson's fans may have been made aware of this only when Willie released his recent homage to pioneering jazz guitarist Django Reinhardt, the all-instrumental disc *Night and Day*, for King, jazz has been his mainstay and true calling throughout his career.

Jackie King's jazz mastery comes to the fore once again on *The Gypsy*, his brand new album, which features his good friend Willie Nelson's inimitable vocals and guitar licks on half of the disc's ten tracks. Described by King as "a love letter to the deep-rooted connection between jazz and country music," the album finds the guitarist within the cozy yet inspiring confines of his regular quintet as together they nimbly swing through a set of choice standards dear to the leader's heart. As Nat Hentoff writes in his liner notes to *The Gypsy*: "Listening to the music here is like being present at an after-hours session among friends who share a mutual interest."

King didn't need much convincing in late 1999 when asked to join Willie Nelson and the Family on tour. He has been part of the close-knit lineup ever since—no easy trick considering the last member of the band hired before King was percussionist Billy English over 15 years ago. Having moved in a decidedly jazzier direction with his *Night and Day* material it was a logical step for Willie to bring another soloist on board, and audiences have responded heartily to the nightly spectacle of their renegade hero swapping leads with his lanky, left-handed guitar ace. The title track of *The Gypsy* has become a regular feature for King in Willie's show, in fact, and the two have even collaborated on a show-stopping new tune, *The Great Divide*, which will kick off Willie's upcoming fall CD release.

"Playing with Jackie every night is a real treat," remarked Nelson. "He's heads above most other guitarists—I mean, I play guitar, but he's a real guitar player. There's a big difference there. Once he gets on the bandstand you know there's a real picker on board, and the whole band has sharpened up since he's joined us. He adds a jazz dimension to what we're doing, and I know there's a real appreciation out there for what he does. When Jackie solos on a chorus, the crowd lets out quite a yell."

JACKIE KING with WILLIE NELSON • THE GYPSY • Indigo Moon / FreeFalls 7014
For media information, interviews etc. contact Brad Riesau at DL Media 610-667-0501
or e-mail: brad.dlmedia@home.com

www.JackieKing.com